Process Reengineering In Action

A Practical Guide To Achieving Breakthrough Results

Richard Y. Chang

Richard Chang Associates, Inc.
Publications Division
Irvine, California

PROCESS REENGINEERING IN ACTION

A Practical Guide To Achieving Breakthrough Results

Richard Y. Chang

Library of Congress Catalog Card Number
94-68228

ISBN 1-883553-16-4

Richard Chang Associates, Inc.
Publications Division
41 Corporate Park, Suite 230
Irvine, CA 92714
(800) 756-8096 • Fax (714) 756-0853

ACKNOWLEDGMENTS

About The Author

Richard Y. Chang is President and CEO of Richard Chang Associates, Inc., a diversified organizational improvement consulting firm based in Irvine, California. He is internationally recognized for his management strategy, quality improvement, organization development, customer satisfaction, and human resource development expertise.

The author would like to acknowledge the support of the entire team of professionals at Richard Chang Associates, Inc. for their contribution to the guidebook development process. In addition, special thanks are extended to the many client organizations who have helped to shape the practical ideas and proven methods shared in this guidebook.

Additional Credits

Editor:	Ruth Stingley and Sarah Ortlieb Fraser
Reviewer:	P. Keith Kelly
Graphic Layout:	Christina Slater
Cover Design:	John Odam Design Associates

PREFACE

The 1990's have already presented individuals and organizations with some very difficult challenges to face and overcome. So who will have the advantage as we move toward the year 2000 and beyond?

The advantage will belong to those with a commitment to continuous learning. Whether on an individual basis or as an entire organization, one key ingredient to building a continuous learning environment is *The Practical Guidebook Collection* brought to you by the Publications Division of Richard Chang Associates, Inc.

After understanding the future *"learning needs"* expressed by our clients and other potential customers, we are pleased to publish *The Practical Guidebook Collection*. These guidebooks are designed to provide you with proven, *"real-world"* tips, tools, and techniques—on a wide range of subjects—that you can apply in the workplace and/or on a personal level immediately.

Once you've had a chance to benefit from *The Practical Guidebook Collection*, please share your feedback with us. We've included a brief *Evaluation and Feedback Form* at the end of the guidebook that you can fax to us at (714) 756-0853.

With your feedback, we can continuously improve the resources we are providing through the Publications Division of Richard Chang Associates, Inc.

Wishing you successful reading,

Richard Y. Chang
President and CEO
Richard Chang Associates, Inc.

TABLE OF CONTENTS

"There's only one corner of the universe you can be certain of improving, and that's your own self."

Aldous Huxley

CHAPTER ONE

INTRODUCTION

Why Read This Guidebook?

For organizations that want to survive, improvement is not an option. It's a given. For organizations that seek to thrive, dramatic improvement is often the only key to success. Small incremental improvements are always necessary, but sometimes quantum leaps are needed if an organization is to forge ahead.

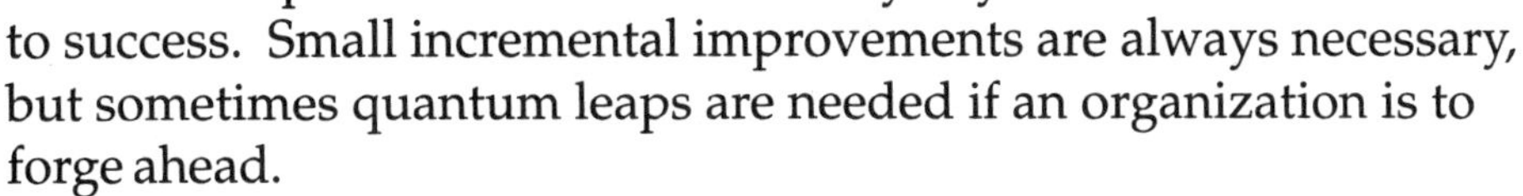

Whether you realize that the old way of doing things needs changing, your customers are demanding a change, or your competitors are taking over your market share, many processes in an organization may need reengineering. Not a minor tweak, but a major overhaul. Perhaps it takes too long for your organization to move products from conception to the marketplace *(and your competitors don't have that problem)*. Maybe your budgeting process is much too complex. It could even be that the services you provide aren't compatible with your customers' needs. It's time to go to the drawing board and start process reengineering.

Process reengineering is a refreshing new approach to doing business. And there is plenty of evidence that it works well —even spectacularly—at times. Performance gains of 100 to 300 percent are common for some reengineered processes.

But process reengineering isn't simple. It takes time, creativity, and a healthy dose of perseverance. You can easily get bogged down with the effort and forget what you're trying to accomplish. Or you can reengineer a process only to discover that the new way isn't much better than the old way. Worse yet, you may find that your reengineered process is more cumbersome or costly than the original process. Some experts estimate that close to 70% of reengineering efforts fail to achieve noticeable results.

This guidebook helps you focus on the essentials to arrive at the right side of process reengineering. If dramatic improvement is your goal, *Process Reengineering In Action* will lead you directly toward it without wasting time on destructive detours. You'll learn to navigate your way toward a process reengineered for success.

Who Should Read This Guidebook?

CEOs and upper-level management are critical players in deciding whether reengineering should take place. But the work of process reengineering is often handed to the managers whose departments will be impacted by the reengineering effort. As well it should. Who knows the shipping process better than the supervisor of shipping? Who, other than the director of finance, understands the budgeting process inside and out? And intuitive managers involve their employees in the reengineering effort, for employees contribute valuable input and may ultimately determine whether the reengineered process is a success.

So whether you're a CEO, a vice president, a member of a reengineering team, a trainer, a manager, a supervisor, or an employee whose work will be impacted by a reengineering effort, you need *Process Reengineering In Action*. It'll take you through the various steps involved with reengineering a process from planning your reengineering effort, to designing changes and implementing them. Each phase builds on the vision and research of the previous phase.

If you are partially or actively involved in a reengineering effort, you can use the practical tips and suggestions provided in this guidebook to plan and gear up for dramatic improvement. You can prepare yourself and others for the change ahead, enabling your organization to transition smoothly. And you can learn how to gauge the success of your venture.

When And How To Use It

If you desire dramatic improvement in one or more processes within your organization, read through this guidebook and apply the Process-Reengineering Model. If you haven't yet begun reengineering a process, follow the model in its entirety. You will learn to successfully plan for, design, and implement a reengineered process.

Perhaps you have already begun reengineering a process. Read through Phases One and Two—the planning and designing phases—and use the tips and tools provided to ensure that you've explored all *"breakthrough"* opportunities. Even if you've just finished a reengineering project, *Process Reengineering In Action* will come in handy. In Phase Three, the implementing phase, you'll learn the importance of implementing on a *"trial-run"* basis and of evaluating your effort to measure its success. And you will be well prepared for your next reengineering effort.

Process reengineering may be your organization's chance to break ahead in an increasingly competitive business arena. Attempt it with the tips and tools in this guidebook. You'll discover that you can accomplish radical improvements successfully.

Note: Many of the other titles from the Practical Guidebook Collection published by Richard Chang Associates, Inc. complement *Process Reengineering In Action*. These include *Continuous Process Improvement, Mastering Change Management, Improving Through Benchmarking, Re-Creating Teams During Transitions, Team Decision-Making Techniques,* and *Continuous Improvement Tools, Volumes 1 and 2,* among others.

WHAT IS PROCESS REENGINEERING?

When engineers tackle a project, they plan, design, and build it. If they were asked to reengineer the same project, they would have to tear it down, then plan, design, and build it all over again. Process reengineering is similar. It requires ripping apart a process and rebuilding it.

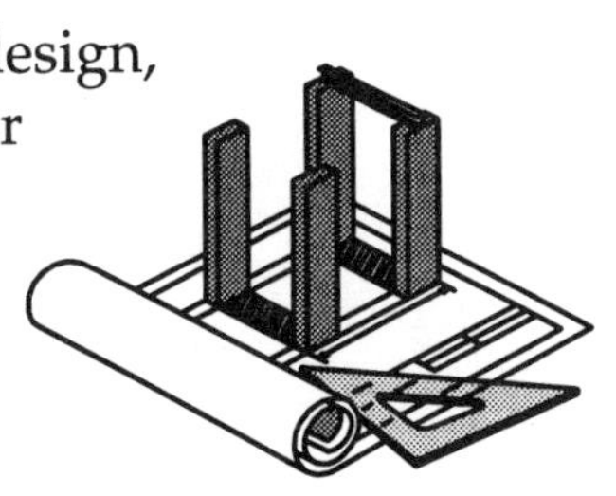

Process reengineering can be defined as:

> The fundamental rethinking and redesigning of existing process tasks and operating structure to achieve dramatic improvements in process performance.

Continuous Process Improvement Versus Process Reengineering

Some organizations shy away from process reengineering, because they feel it's too costly and too time-consuming. *"Why scrap a process,"* they say, *"when we can try to fix it instead?"* Their point is well taken. Why attempt surgery when an antiseptic and a bandage would work just as well? The answer is to investigate and appraise the problem. A cut can be bandaged; a cancer requires more drastic measures. You need to determine whether a certain process within your organization requires minor healing *(continuous process improvement)* or major surgery *(process reengineering)*.

Both continuous process improvement *(referred to as CPI)* and process reengineering are necessary to drive *"breakthroughs" (significant advances)* in organizational performance, but they differ in a number of ways.

The differences include:

Management Involvement

CPI typically involves employees at all levels and emphasizes continuous incremental improvement of work processes. Process reengineering typically involves managers in a more *"hands-on"* role, since process reengineering often leads to changing organizational structure and redesigning jobs.

Intensity Of Team Member Involvement

CPI involves team members on an *"as needed,"* part-time basis over an extended time frame. Process reengineering requires much more intense team member involvement, often on a regular, full-time basis over a condensed time frame.

Improvement Goals

CPI results in the achievement of successive incremental improvements over a period of time, starting from how a work process currently operates and improving upon it. Process reengineering is periodic and focuses on the achievement of dramatic improvement, radically redesigning how a process operates without being constrained by how things were previously being done.

Implementation Approach

CPI builds on making incremental improvements that add up to significant improvements overall for an organization. Process reengineering focuses on outcome and on making breakthrough improvements at one time, instead of adding up the sum of multiple gains.

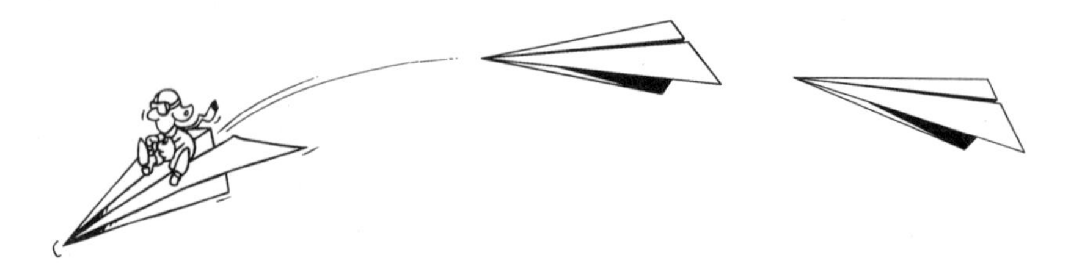

Magnitude Of Organizational Change

With CPI, organizational changes happen over an extended period of time, often with limited disruption to existing jobs, management systems, and organizational structures. With process reengineering, radical process changes often go hand in hand with changes in job design, management systems, training and retraining, organizational structure, and information technology.

Extent Of Focus

CPI usually focuses on narrowly defined processes, which often involve frontline employees who are working to improve a subprocess that is part of a higher-level process. Process reengineering needs to focus on broad-based, cross-functional processes that span the larger part of an entire organizational system.

Dependence Upon Information Systems

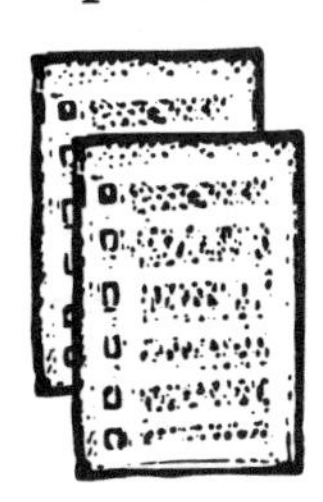

Organizations that use only CPI occasionally find themselves reinventing the *"paper trail"* by redesigning a form, creating a new piece of correspondence, etc. With process reengineering, information systems technology often helps pave the way to radical improvements in cycle-time reduction, information access, and paper trail elimination.

Organizations that value improvement should get in the habit of encouraging or even mandating employee input on improvement opportunities. Employees should look at every process with improvement potential in mind. An organization should train its employees to continually ask themselves the questions on the following page.

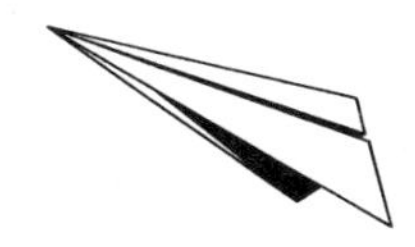

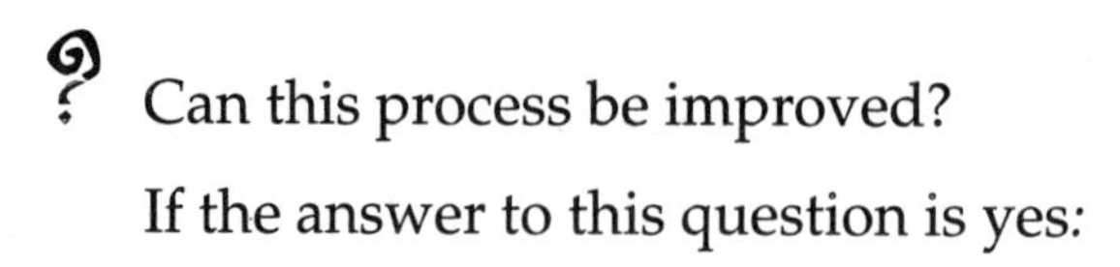

Can this process be improved?

If the answer to this question is yes:

What is the best way to do this process with the tools and skills that we have? *(CPI)*

—or—

Will improvement require a dramatic change? *(Process reengineering)*

It's often the employees *(or suppliers of a process)* who have their fingers on the pulse of an organization's opportunities for breakthrough improvements. If an organization conditions its employees to routinely question the capabilities of any process in which they're involved and responds to their suggestions, then they will foster an atmosphere of creativity and opportunity.

Both CPI and process reengineering have a place in today's organizations. In fact, CPI should be a mainstay in every organization. Process reengineering, on the other hand, is necessary at certain times in certain situations. At those times, CPI isn't adequate for the job.

Deciding Which Approach To Use

Your employees can provide valuable insights into improvement opportunities and whether they can be accomplished through CPI or process reengineering. Other key considerations when deciding which approach to use include:

Marketplace Changes

If the marketplace for your products and/or services is undergoing rapid changes, making incremental improvements to existing processes may be fueling a slow death. Under this circumstance, reengineering a broadly defined business process *(e.g., New Product/Service Development)* may be more appropriate.

Geographic Spread

If the process is typically *"housed"* within one or two physical locations *(e.g., work groups/departments, etc.)* and data exchange or hand-off is not critical, then CPI may be best. However, with processes spanning multiple locations *(particularly crossing states and/or countries)* and requiring critical data exchange, reengineering may be best.

Customer/Supplier Involvement

If a relatively low degree of *"hands-on"* customer and supplier involvement is desired *(or even possible since accessibility is an issue)*, then CPI may be most appropriate. A reengineering approach typically demands a greater degree of direct involvement with key customers and suppliers of the process being reengineered.

Cost And Staffing Allocation

If top management is only willing to dedicate limited financial resources and periodic, part-time involvement of those involved, then consider taking a CPI approach. Part-time reengineering efforts have commonly resulted in limited resources, increased frustration on the part of team members, and missed expectations on the part of senior management.

Level Of Urgency

Organizations that are relatively low on the quality improvement *"maturity curve"* may find that gradually and continually improving a process is the best approach for them. Reengineering is more appropriate if an existing process is failing or when the situation is drastic and significant improvement must be achieved in a relatively short period of time.

Core Elements Of Process Reengineering

Process reengineering is much more complex than CPI. That is why it is more demanding, more time-consuming, and usually more costly. The upside is that it can result in great rewards for both your organization and its employees.

Consider, for example, an organization that invests resources in reengineering the way customer service representatives handle customer complaints. The organization purchases new hardware and software, redesigns jobs, and trains the reps. The effort takes eight months from start to finish, but the payoff is tremendous. The customer-service index jumps dramatically upward, a greater number of customers become repeat customers, and the turnover of customer service reps drops. It's a win-win situation.

Process reengineering is more complex and results in drastic improvement because it affects change in more than one area. To achieve breakthrough organizational performance, process reengineering usually drives change in three different areas. These areas are:

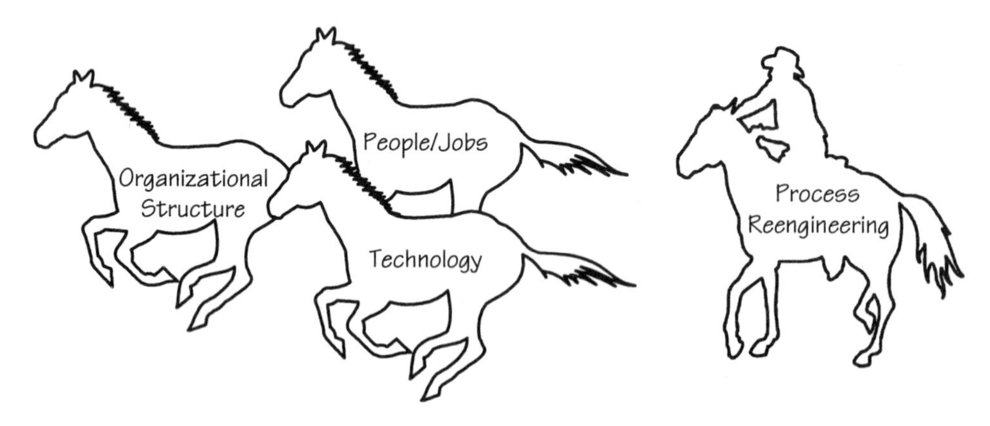

Process reengineering does more than look into improvement concerns. It attempts radical change through organizational restructuring, work redesigning, and technological retooling. These three *"core elements"* of reengineering are the backbone of its success.

Organizational restructuring

Organizations that remain structured *"the same way"* after a reengineering effort as they were before one, may have difficulty overcoming the business issues and marketplace challenges that drove them into a reengineering effort in the first place. Some form of restructuring is often a key ingredient of a reengineering effort. When restructuring your organization, you need to consider:

- Reducing organizational layers
- Realigning functions/work groups around the customer
- Driving accountability to the front line

Work redesigning

Work is typically designed so that a particular employee has responsibility *(and possibly accountability)* for portions of an entire work process. Such a design often builds in inherent *"in-process"* hand-off delays, lack of accountability for the ultimate process outcome, and increased needs for supervision. When redesigning work in your organization, you will need to consider:

- Conducting a *"customer value-added"* process analysis of job tasks
- Expanding job scope and ownership
- Building cross-functional teams

Technological retooling

Simply computerizing the old methods for doing things will not necessarily eliminate performance deficiencies or drive radical improvements in process productivity and capability. Technological retooling for optimum performance through reengineering requires that you consider:

- Increasing the emphasis on process tasks that happen in parallel
- Gathering and communicating customer-related data
- Expediting access to information and data for all employees

Understanding the improvement opportunities and challenges that underlie process reengineering is the first step in discovering whether it can work successfully in your organization at this particular time. It's a critical decision. If you're willing to pursue the route to dramatic improvement, read on.

Chapter Two Worksheet: Looking For Improvement Opportunities

Based upon your own experiences and perceptions *(preferably with your present organization)*, please respond to the following questions.

1. What *"major challenges" (from a quality improvement, business performance, and/or operational perspective)* do you anticipate your organization will be facing between now and the year 2000?

____

____

____

2. What *"specific obstacles/limitations"* do you anticipate your organization will need to overcome in order to prepare its workforce for successfully addressing/overcoming the above-listed challenges?

____

____

____

3. How can process reengineering help you to overcome the above-listed obstacles/limitations?

____

____

____

APPLYING A PROCESS-REENGINEERING MODEL

Not every process-reengineering effort will look the same, follow the same path, or result in the same payoff, which is not unusual. Children from the same parents that are raised in the same environment are not carbon copies of each other. They may require different parenting styles.

Likewise, you can't presume that there is only one *"right"* way to approach process reengineering. However, just as parents can follow certain guidelines that make parenting easier and less stressful, you can also use guidelines to approach your process-reengineering effort.

Think of it this way. If you were to build a model airplane, you would use the materials provided and follow the directions to achieve the same sleek airplane pictured on the box. But what if you had different materials to work with? By following the same basic directions you could create an airplane. Some of the directions might not apply to the materials you choose, and your airplane might look quite different, but at least you'd be ahead of someone who didn't have any directions.

Given a choice, would you rather attempt an effort on your own *(without help)* or follow the advice of others who had achieved success? Maybe it seems an obvious choice, but some people would rather risk organizational suicide to prove that they can do it alone. You wouldn't be reading this guidebook if you were in that group. Congratulations! You want to improve your chances of making breakthrough improvements in your organization.

The Process-Reengineering Model

The Process-Reengineering Model that follows gives you guidelines that will pave the way for your reengineering effort. Spend as much time as you feel is necessary on each step in the three phases. Organizations with complex processes that cross many functions may find it necessary to plan far more thoroughly than organizations with simpler processes.

The Process-Reengineering Model

PLAN

DESIGN

IMPLEMENT

1. Determine "*New*" Process Requirements

2. Uncover "*Breakthrough*" Opportunities

3. Map The "*Ideal*" Process

4. Redefine Process Support Requirements

5. Develop Change Management Plan

6. Implement On "*Trial Run*" Basis

7. Standardize The Reengineered Process

8. Evaluate Process Performance On An Ongoing Basis

Phase One — P

Phase Two — D

Phase Three — I

Revisions

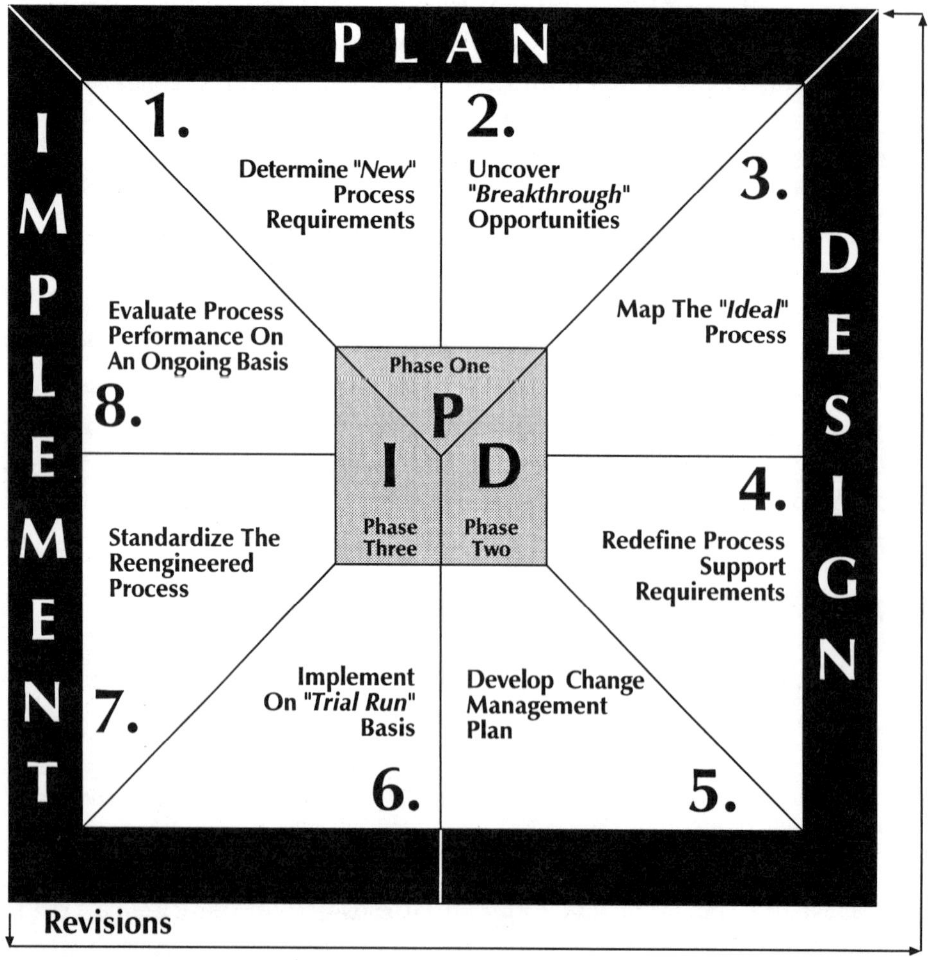

The Process-Reengineering Model is structured around three phases—planning, designing, and implementing. Each of the three phases contains major steps that direct you toward making the most of your reengineering effort. The following chart identifies the phases and their major steps.

Phase One: Plan

Determine *"New"* Process Requirements

Uncover *"Breakthrough"* Opportunities

- Analyze *"as is"* capability
- Envision desired state
- Identify process performance *"gaps"*

Phase Two: Design

Map The *"Ideal"* Process

- Complete preliminary work
- Set new goals and establish measures
- Create a new process flow chart

Redefine Process Support Requirements

Develop Change Management Plan

Phase Three: Implement

Implement On *"Trial Run"* Basis

Standardize The Reengineered Process

Evaluate Process Performance On An Ongoing Basis

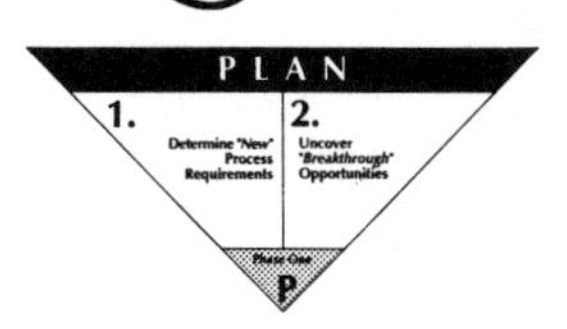

In Phase One of the Process-Reengineering Model—the planning phase, you will take a close look at the process you want to reengineer. You'll forecast the requirements for the *"new"* process by focusing on customers' current and future needs, analyzing what the old process is currently accomplishing, creating a vision of what you want the reengineered process to achieve, and zeroing in on the differences between the two. When you finish this phase of the Process-Reengineering Model, you should have a good grip on reality. If your planning results in a great desire to change, you will tackle the next phase.

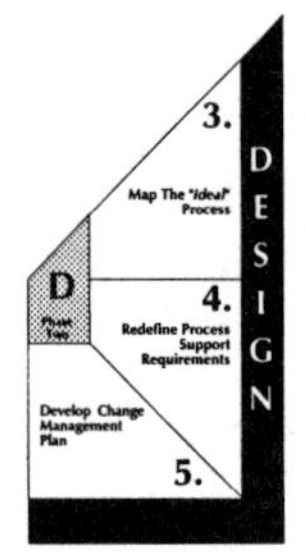

Phase Two, which involves designing a reengineered process, takes you from the actual mapping of the new process to the development of a change management plan. In between these two steps, you will be redefining and redesigning jobs, taking a careful look at the technology available, and considering your organization's resources. If you do your homework in this phase, then the last phase will run a lot smoother.

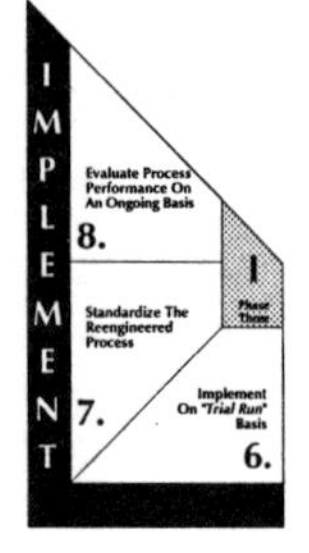

Finally, in Phase Three, which involves implementing a reengineered process, you'll be testing out the new process, encouraging commitment to it, and gauging its success. And you'll work toward promoting an atmosphere of continuous process improvement in which employees strive to make improvements that make a difference to the customer.

Sound simple? Hardly. But it's definitely worthwhile if your organization desires or needs to make great leaps of improvement. Follow along in this guidebook as one organization, Shore Up, Inc., undertakes process reengineering.

Selecting A Process Reengineering Team

The true starting point of a process reengineering effort is putting together a team of people who will drive the effort. You should consider several factors when designing a team and selecting members, such as:

- Should there be an interim team with the mandate of looking at the need for reengineering first?
- Should the team manage the process reengineering effort from beginning to end?
- Should team members be assigned to the team for the entire duration or just come and go as needed?
- Should team members be selected for their first-hand knowledge of the process being reengineered, their authority level, or for other reasons?
- Should the team be made up of a small core group, or should it bring together a larger group of people who have contributions to make?
- How much autonomy should the team have?

The answers to these questions and others relating to team design will depend on the scope of the process being reengineered, the effort involved, and who needs to have input, among other factors. One of the most important issues at this stage is the decision regarding team size and structure.

Here are a couple of the many options you might be looking at:

"Core Team" Approach

- small team—three or four members
- strong commitment from these core members
- large percentage of their time devoted to the reengineering *(full, or nearly full time)*
- selected for their ability to self-manage
- bring in others as needed

Pros:

- A small team can often move more quickly and achieve results faster than a larger group.
- Members are more committed to the task because of deeper involvement.
- Others who have contributions do not need to be pulled from their regular responsibilities until they are actually needed.

Cons:

- The team may not have all the skills on board.
- There is the risk that the team becomes *"isolated"* from the rest of the organization.

"Full Team" Approach

- larger team—eight to twelve or even more members
- made up of those involved in the process, as well as process suppliers and customers
- members' participation is usually part-time *(approximately 10 to 25% of their time)*
- members stay on the team as the reengineering effort moves forward
- selected for their ability to make a specific contribution to the team

Pros:

Cons:

Pros:

- Most or all of the skills and input are built into the team at its creation.
- The team typically has contacts and resources available in various parts of the organization.

Cons:

- It may not move as quickly as a smaller group.
- Some team members may feel the reengineering effort is not that important if it is being handled by a *"committee"* type of group.
- More effort is required to manage and coordinate a larger group, deflecting energy from the task at hand—process reengineering.

Obviously, there are options in between these two as well. And don't forget, you may end up changing the team as you progress, adapting to the situation at hand. However you go about designing the team and selecting its members, make sure the team has a clear picture of where they are going, and they are all following the same path to get there—the Process Reengineering Model.

A Case Example: Shore Up, Inc.

Shore Up, Inc. a mail-order company..., began selling casual clothing made from 100% organic cotton for children and adults eighteen years ago, and over the years slowly added handmade gift items and unique toys to their catalogue. Customers, recognizing the quality of Shore Up's clothing and the individuality of their gifts and toys, often become repeat buyers. But recently Shore Up has begun to run into some major obstacles.

Over the past two years, Shore Up has been working on improving a number of work processes within the company in order to meet customer requirements. However, customer complaints have increased rather than decreased in the last year. Mark Reilly, owner and CEO of Shore Up, began looking into the complaints, which mainly centered around dissatisfaction with timely receipt of purchases and the inability of customer service representatives to solve problems related to order fulfillment. Mark hired Loudin, an outside consultant, to help identify where and how Shore Up could improve in this area.

Mark and Loudin asked Shelley, the customer service manager, and Joshua, the senior order-entry clerk, to join them in analyzing the problem. Both Shelley and Joshua provided insights. *"Customers want their merchandise immediately,"* Shelley said. *"Eighteen years ago, when Shore Up started, it was okay to deliver in two weeks. Today, two weeks is way too long. We received so many complaints from customers who didn't receive gifts in time this past holiday season."* Joshua nodded. *"And when the customers call,"* he added, *"they want to know if we have a particular item in stock. We don't have the capability to provide that information while they are waiting on the phone."*

Together the team delved into the complaints and gathered additional input from employees in customer service, order entry, shipping, inventory, and catalogue production. *"I suggest you seriously consider reengineering the process,"* Loudin said. *"Reengineering the order fulfillment process could very well be the only way you'll resolve customer dissatisfaction and come out ahead. But it will take a lot of commitment on your part. Are you up for it?"*

Mark agreed to the process-reengineering project. *"But I'd like more input from the customers,"* he said. *"That's a given,"* Loudin responded. *"It's one of the first steps we'll take in the process."*

Stay tuned as Shore Up, using a *"core team"* approach, follows the steps in the Process-Reengineering Model in hopes of achieving breakthrough improvements.

CHAPTER THREE WORKSHEET: CONSIDERING PROCESS REENGINEERING?

1. Describe the process you're considering to reengineer.

____

____

2. What forces are driving you to consider reengineering *(e.g., customer demands, marketplace changes, level of urgency, etc.)*?

____

____

____

3. Describe your organization's commitment to and support for reengineering?

____

____

4. List the different functional areas your process-reengineering effort will impact *(e.g., customer service, finance, shipping, etc.)*.

____

____

____

DETERMINE "NEW" PROCESS REQUIREMENTS

Phase One: Plan Your Reengineering Effort

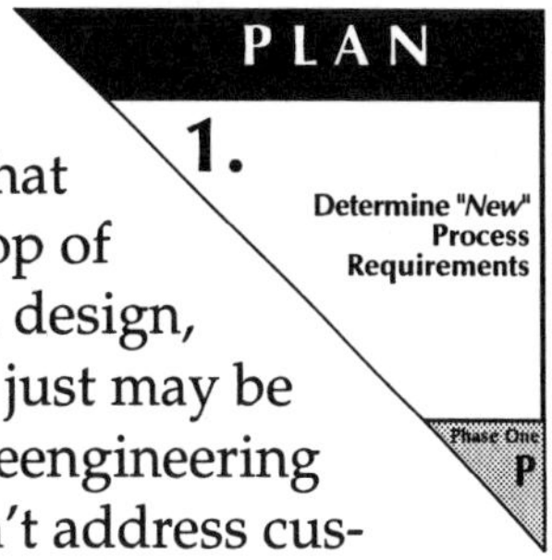

You initially have decided that reengineering a process will benefit your organization. Change is lurking in the near future, change that will send organizational performance to the top of the charts. If, that is, you thoroughly plan for, design, and implement your reengineered process. It just may be that you discover in the planning phase that reengineering this process won't add value. Or that it doesn't address customer needs. Or that you don't have the resources to do what you'd like. That's why this phase is so critical.

The first step in the planning phase requires that you roll up your sleeves and dig into what reengineering this process demands. Determining *"new"* process requirements involves uncovering what customers and the marketplace require of your process, and focusing in on your own operating requirements. That's where you have to start. This information will fuel other decisions you have to make regarding your reengineering effort.

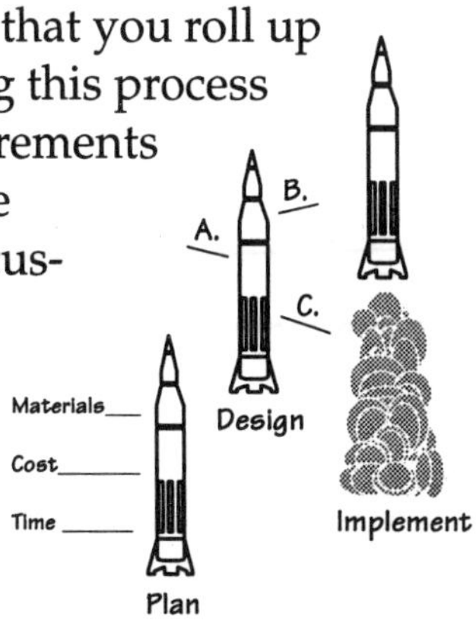

What Do Your Customers Want?

Successful reengineering projects realign processes to satisfy customer demands. Are you in tune with what your customers want? Or have you banked on the fact that they were satisfied and now you're facing major business declines? Organizations that undergo process reengineering report that the standard credo of *"the customer comes first"* hits home. If it does for your organization, you're in the game. If it doesn't, you might as well hand in your glove.

Identifying your customers

Before you can determine what your customers want, you have to know who the customers of your process are. *"That's easy,"* you say. Certainly it is if your customers are external, but what if you have to search for internal customers in an organization that has many departments whose employees perform interrelated tasks? Then the task becomes a bit more difficult.

Work with your process-reengineering team to brainstorm a list of external and internal customers *"for the process"* being reengineered. Don't be afraid to list anyone who comes to mind. Ask your team members two key questions:

- Who is affected by this process?
- Who depends on this process for information, products or service?

Zeroing in on customer concerns

Once you've identified your customers, you need to zero in on what concerns them. If you're already aware of their concerns, it'll be much easier to develop interviewing instruments. Brainstorm with your team members what you think your customers require of the process you're attempting to reengineer.

Customer *"requirement areas"* often encompass some of the following:

- timeliness
- cost
- accuracy
- functionality
- responsiveness
- follow-through
- quantity
- thoroughness
- dimension
- yield
- price
- availability

The process-reengineering team...

at Shore Up identified the external buying customer as the most important customer to satisfy. *"But we have quite a few internal customers involved in taking and filling orders,"* Shelley said. *"What about the customer service department and order-entry clerks?"* Joshua broke in with, *"And don't forget the shipping department and even those in the billing department. A lot of people are involved in this process."*

"Well, since we're most concerned about the buying customer," Loudin began, *"let's figure out what those custòmers need or expect from us."* Together the team decided that the customers were interested in the following requirements within the order-fulfillment process *(based on experience and customer interactions):*

- timely delivery
- knowledgeable clerks and representatives
- availability of clerks and representatives
- receiving correct merchandise

Although these were broad areas, the team could begin to formulate questions for the customers. The survey forms, then, would help them gather information about specific customer needs and expectations....

Soliciting customer input

You've identified your customers and zeroed in on their areas of concern. Now you're in the position to develop interview/survey questions and solicit customer input. Design questions that relate to the areas that concern your customers. Ask for enough input to help you gather data and measure customer needs and expectations, but don't go overboard. Your customers will appreciate the fact that you consider their time valuable.

After you produce your questionnaire, interview your customers. Encourage their participation and thank them for their time. If you interview or survey a good representation of your customers, you should be able to gather key information that will aid your process-reengineering effort.

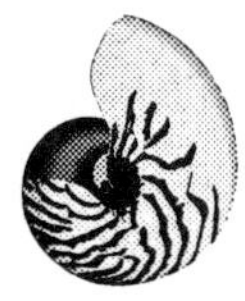

Shore Up's process-reengineering team..., along with the help of a few employees from finance, shipping, and catalogue production, devised a satisfaction survey for their customers. Here is a sample of the survey they created.

Shore Up, Inc. Satisfaction Survey

The purpose of this survey is to evaluate how well Shore Up, Inc. is serving its customers and to target specific areas for improvement. Your candid responses will be invaluable in our efforts to increase customer satisfaction.

Instructions

Each statement will require two responses from you. In the first box write in the number that indicates **the extent to which you agree** with each statement. Then, for the same statement, write in the number in the second box indicating **how important this area is to you.**

Please mark the **extent to which you agree** box as follows:
(**1**) Strongly Disagree, (**2**) Disagree, (**3**) Neutral, (**4**) Agree,
(**5**) Strongly Agree, and (**NO**) No Opinion.

Please mark the **how important this area is to you** box as follows: (**1**) Not Important, (**2**) Slightly Important, (**3**) Somewhat Important, (**4**) Important, (**5**) Very Important, and (**NO**) No Opinion.

Example: Shore Up's "1-800" number is easy to remember.	AGREE	IMPORTANCE
	5	2

As you can see, this person *strongly agrees* with this statement and wrote a "5" in the Agree box. However, this person feel it is only *slightly important* to being satisfied as a Shore Up customer and wrote "2" in the Importance box.

26. What is the single most important element affecting your satisfaction with our services? *(Please check only one.)*

- ☐ Phone calls are answered quickly
- ☐ Attitude of service representatives
- ☐ Timely order delivery
- ☐ Merchandise availability
- ☐ Accuracy in processing my order
- ☐ Other *(please specify)* ____________________

Thank you for your participation. Please return this survey in the enclosed self-addressed envelope.

Shore Up distributed over 6,000 surveys...

randomly inserted in their next catalogue mailing. To encourage returns, they enclosed a coupon for 10% off each customer's next order. Their response rate was 42%. The process-reengineering team tabulated the results and discovered that Shore Up's customers wanted:

- Their merchandise shipped in a much more timely manner
- Service representatives who could track their orders *(currently they couldn't)*
- Easier order forms
- Easier phone ordering *(more convenient hours, less waiting for available reps, more information regarding stock on hand)*

On the plus side, Shore Up was fulfilling customer needs in the areas of shipping correct merchandise and supplying accurate shipping forms. And, although phone representatives couldn't always resolve problems on first contact, they were perceived as being courteous....

Knowing what your customers want helps you reengineer a process correctly. After all, you shouldn't undertake process reengineering just because the CEO thinks the process should be done differently or because your biggest competitor is reengineering a process *(and you have yet to see the results)*. If your customers want something more than you can currently deliver, that's your first clue. Find out what they want before proceeding with your plan.

It's also helpful to forecast future customer requirements. If you're going to tear apart a process and rebuild it, wouldn't you rather rebuild it to achieve breakthrough performance for twenty years instead of ten? Ask your customers what they would like to see you provide down the line. If it's possible to work it into your reengineering effort, do it.

What Is The Marketplace Providing?

How does your organization compare with the competition? Are you above the rest? Or are you struggling to keep up? Take a good look at what your competitors offer. If your customers have already picked up on a discrepancy, you'll know that your process must change. If a competing fast-food restaurant is offering super-low prices or super-fast service, and the customers are flocking to their restaurant instead of yours, then you might opt for process reengineering so you can offer the same incentive.

Maybe your customers are quite satisfied with the process you're considering reengineering, but they won't be for long, because the competition is doing it so much better. This goes hand in hand with forecasting future customer requirements. Don't wait until it's too late, and you lose customers to your competitors. Stay abreast of what's happening in the marketplace.

New-product development is a process that lends itself well to reengineering. If your competitors continually offer new products much faster than you do, start looking at process reengineering. Or maybe you debut new products soon after development, but they flop because not enough research has been completed or you've shortcut your marketing analyses.

To keep up with what the marketplace offers:

- Know what's out there (don't live in a bubble)
- Keep a close eye on your competitors
- Be open to new ideas, services, and/or products

Using benchmarking

Knowing that other organizations are doing better than you is one thing. Knowing how they do it better is quite different. Benchmarking can provide you with the inside information you need to reengineer a process. Benchmarking involves learning and discovering how other work groups within your organization perform common processes or how other competitive or world-class organizations operate. You choose successful operations and try to adapt their processes to your own.

Benchmarking is especially critical to any process-reengineering effort, because it provides goals to shoot for and aids in helping you envision and design your new process. Whether you survey other organizations by phone, read about them in business literature, or visit them to observe and analyze, focus on how their process(es) run and what measures are in place. It'll put you far ahead in your reengineering effort.

Shore Up realized that marketplace...

requirements had changed. Over the past two years, they had made some strides in responding to the new demands *(e.g., phone ordering and a 1-800 number, computer installation for order entry, credit card purchases, etc.),* but they still fell behind, because of the *"mail-order mentality." "We're still doing things the same way we did eighteen years ago,"* Joshua observed. *"Not exactly,"* Shelley said. *"We are computer-automated now."*

"That served a purpose at a certain time," Loudin began, *"but now you're no longer just a mail-order company. Shore Up receives more phone orders than mail orders, but you still ship merchandise the same way. Your competitors promise shipping within 24 hours of receipt of most orders. You're still operating under the guidelines set nearly two decades ago. Times have changed."*

"You're absolutely right," Mark responded. *"Our customers aren't happy with the way things are. It's high time we reengineered this process."* Loudin asked, *"Have you ever benchmarked other companies?"*

They hadn't, so Loudin explained the purpose of benchmarking. *"You don't have to observe a direct competitor,"* he said. *"Why not pinpoint some successful mail-order companies that sell different products and are recognized for having high performing order-fulfillment processes?"* Mark thought that was a great idea and committed to contacting and observing other companies. *"I'll work with you on it,"* Loudin offered....

What Are Your Operating Requirements?

When you know what your customers want and you've identified what the marketplace offers, you're ready to look at what you need to achieve to meet the wants and demands of those driving your reengineering effort. Do you need to reduce costs so you can offer price reductions to your customers? Do you need to become more technology-based so that you can get rid of the excess paper that's clogging up your organization? Or do you need to reduce the number of times an order is touched?

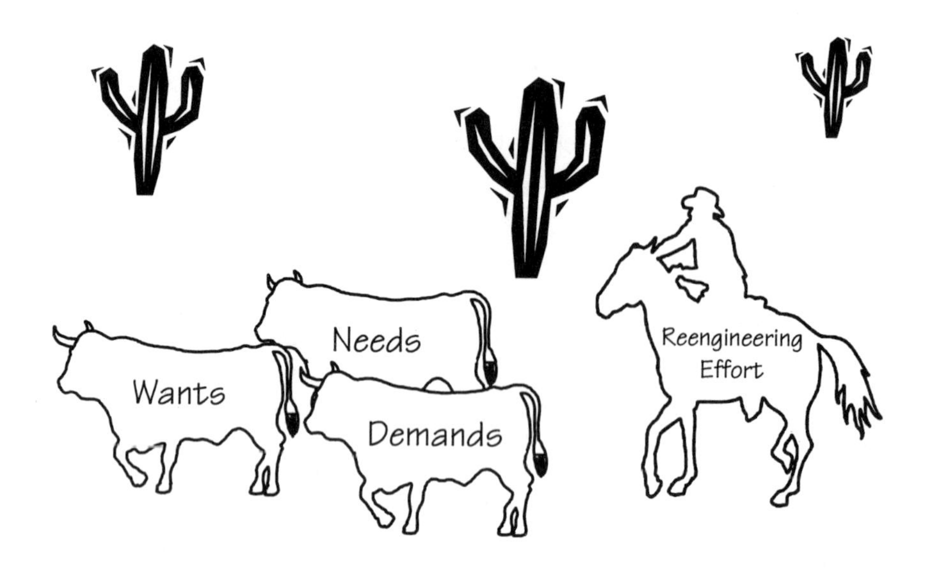

What does your organization expect the reengineered process to do? Brainstorm with your team and identify what the process should do based on the customer and marketplace information you've gathered. Be specific. How much should costs be reduced? Ten percent? Fifty? Should only two managers be required to okay an order, or will one or no approval save you necessary time? Will you need to purchase computer hardware and software that runs marketing reports you formulated by hand?

Shore Up's process-reengineering team...

identified operating requirements they felt were needed. *"Our first and primary requirement should be to reduce shipping time,"* Mark stated. *"The marketplace demands it, and our customers are becoming disgruntled because it takes too long to get orders."* Loudin stepped in. *"Be specific. What are your requirements for shipping time?"* he asked. *"I think we should ship within twenty-four hours, unless it's a special order that will take more time. Then we'll be on the same performance level as our competitors,"* Mark said. *"Shouldn't we design our process to be faster than our competitors? The three companies I observed shipped within twenty-four hours. And one used a scanner for mail order forms. That reduced order-entry time considerably. I think we should do the same."* The team continued to discuss their options and identify other operating requirements.

Determining new process requirements involves researching what your customers want and what the marketplace offers, and determining what operating requirements you need to set for the *"new"* process to meet those demands. Completing this step of the planning phase should provide insight into the forces behind your effort and prepare you to move forward.

Chapter Four Worksheet: Focusing On Your Customers

1. List the key customer(s) of the process you want to reengineer.

2. Briefly summarize the concerns of your key customer(s).

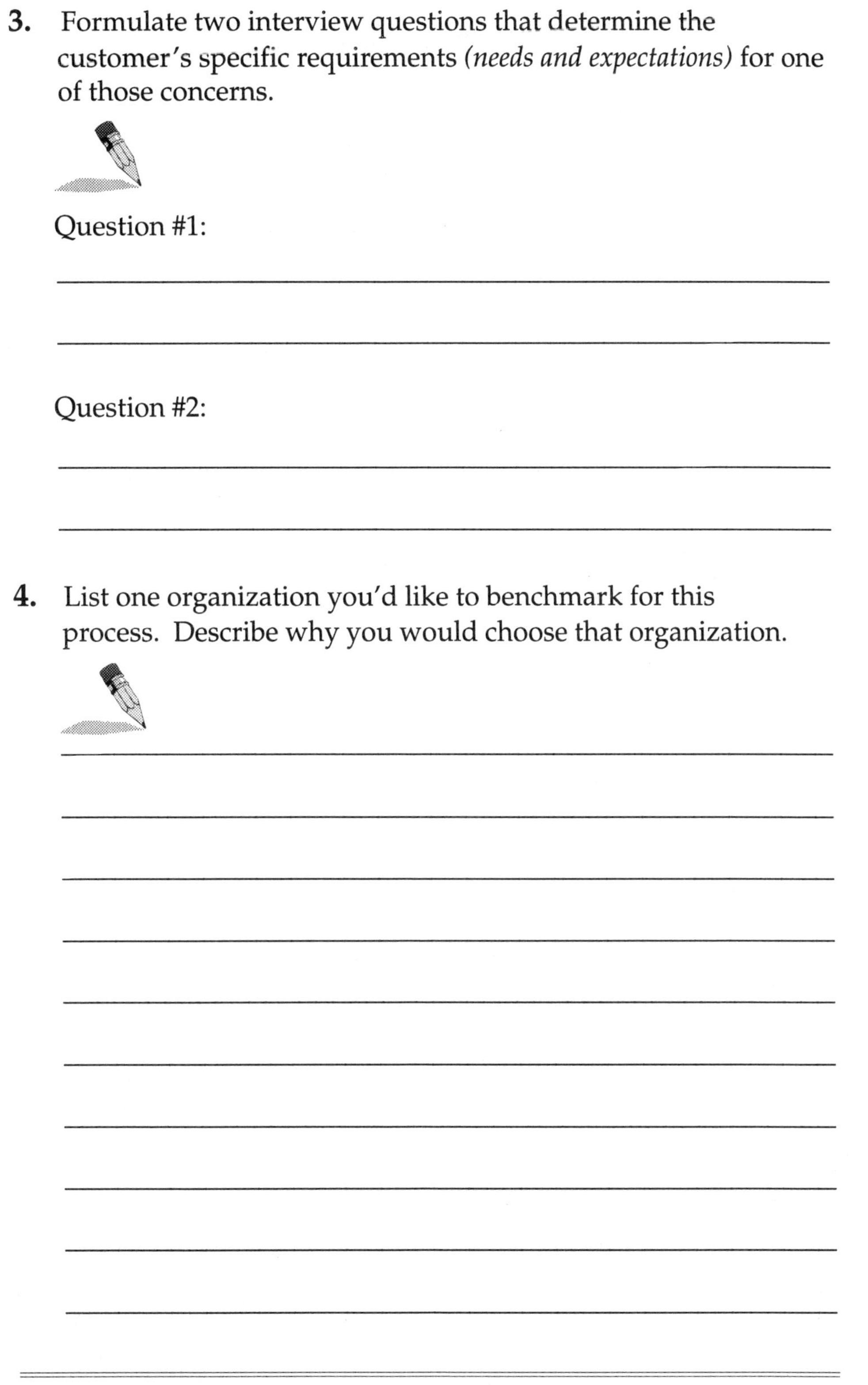

3. Formulate two interview questions that determine the customer's specific requirements *(needs and expectations)* for one of those concerns.

Question #1:

Question #2:

4. List one organization you'd like to benchmark for this process. Describe why you would choose that organization.

UNCOVER *"BREAKTHROUGH"* OPPORTUNITIES

PLAN

2.
Uncover
"Breakthrough"
Opportunities

Phase One
P

Are you ready to discover if process reengineering will help your organization scale great heights of performance improvement? This step in the planning phase can be very exciting if the information you uncover points you toward that possibility. You will look at your current process to determine what it is accomplishing, create a vision of what the *"new process"* should be like, and figure out the difference between the two.

Performance Improvement

All conjectures will either be backed by solid research or will be replaced with factual evidence. Your guesswork will be transformed into practical suggestions that lead you toward exceptional leaps in process and organizational performance. To uncover breakthrough opportunities, you will need to do the following:

- Analyze "As Is" Capability
- Envision Desired State, and
- Identify Process Performance "Gaps"

Desired State

Analyze *"As Is"* Capability

Unless you know how the process is currently performing, you can't state with any degree of certainty whether or not process reengineering will benefit your organization. Maybe you've decided that you want to reengineer the process of washing cars in your car-wash business because you think it takes too long, and you want to increase profitability by having the capacity to wash more cars per hour.

You begin to reengineer the process so that each car receiving a machine wash, wax, vacuuming, and buffing by hand is finished within ten minutes. Process reengineering helps you reach your goal of ten minutes per car. But had you measured your original process, you would have discovered that it only took ten and a half minutes.

Okay, so you think you're not as obtuse as the car-wash reengineering team. But say the car-wash team had measured the original process and were able to reduce the time to six minutes. In the reengineering process, however, they forgot to figure out the cost of labor. The end result is that profitability decreases, because they had to hire additional help to speed up the time. Now if the goal was time reduction because customers demanded it *(and profitability wasn't a factor)*, then the effort could be considered successful. But process reengineering is usually quite complex. All major aspects of a process must be defined and then measured to achieve the greatest breakthroughs.

Begin by documenting the *"as is"* process. You need to define and map out all the tasks in the process. By doing so, you will have a clear and realistic view of the process. It will also provide you with information that will help when you begin the designing phase. The two basic steps involved in documenting a process are:

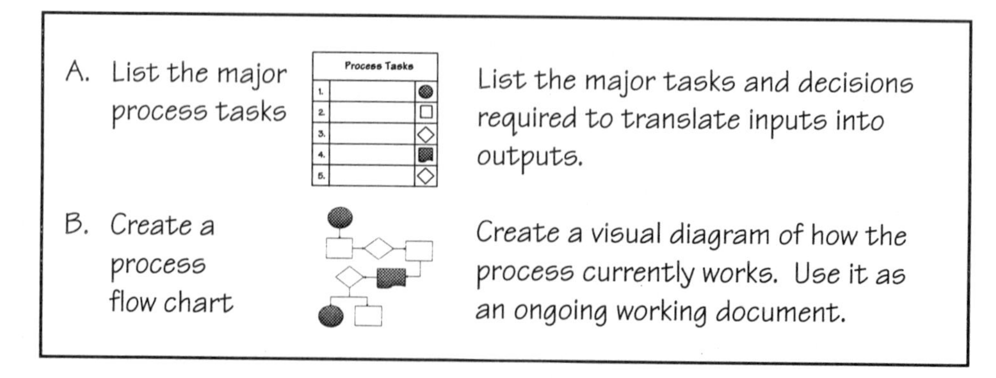

List the major process tasks

First, determine what is the input and the output involved in the process. If you are analyzing the process of preparing market reports, the input would be the gathered data; the output would be the actual reports. Everything in between would be the tasks involved in the process.

Next, list the major tasks and their decision points. And after the major tasks have been identified, determine what smaller subtasks and decisions link the major tasks together. Ask yourself questions along the way to help with this section of analyzing *"as is"* capability. Possible questions include:

- What really happens next?
- Does someone need to make a decision before this task?
- What approvals are required before proceeding?
- Is there anything missing in these tasks?

Shore Up's process-reengineering team...

began brainstorming the tasks involved in the order-fulfillment process. *"What's the input?"* Loudin asked. *"Wouldn't the input be the order?"* Joshua asked. *"And the output would be the merchandise arriving at the customer's door,"* he added. *"I agree with Joshua,"* Shelley stated, *"but the process differs for mail and telephone orders. Mail orders go into the bins and are accompanied by payment; phone orders are directly keyed into the computer and are charged."*

"Good point," Loudin responded. *"So we currently fill out two different forms, one for phone and one for mail orders."* Together the team began to identify the tasks and subtasks involved in the order-fulfillment process at Shore Up....

Create a process flow chart

Creating a process flow chart allows you to visually see what happens at each step of the process. Try to limit the detail in your flow chart. For example, if you were listing or flow charting the tasks involved in a car wash process, you wouldn't include minor details, such as opening the door, inserting the key in the ignition, releasing the break, etc. Too much detail defeats your purpose.

Decide on which symbols you want to use in your flow chart. Some of the more common symbols used in flow charts include:

SYMBOL	NAME	EXPLANATION
(rounded rectangle)	Elongated Circle	Shows the starting and ending points of a flow chart.
(rectangle)	Box	Any workflow task. Each box should contain a short description of the task being performed.
(diamond)	Diamond	Any decision point. Each diamond should contain a question that can be answered *"yes"* or *"no."*
Ⓐ	Connector	A small circle with a letter is used to connect one task of a flow chart to another.
(document shape)	Document	A transfer *(or output)* of a hard copy document.
(zigzag arrow)	Zigzag Arrow	Shows an electronic data transfer.
→	Straight Arrow	Shows direction of process flow.

The process-reengineering team at Shore Up...

took the items on their process task list and drew a flow chart. Here's the flow chart they created for the order-fulfillment process:

Process: Order Fulfillment

TASK #	MAJOR PROCESS TASKS	SUBTASKS/DECISIONS	SYMBOL
1	Customer service rep receives order		
1a		By phone?	
1b		Customer service rep writes info on order form	
1c		By mail or fax?	
1d		Customer service rep verifies order form	
1e		Corrections made as appropriate	
2	Forward form to order-entry clerk		
3	Order-entry clerk key enters data		
14	File copy of invoice		

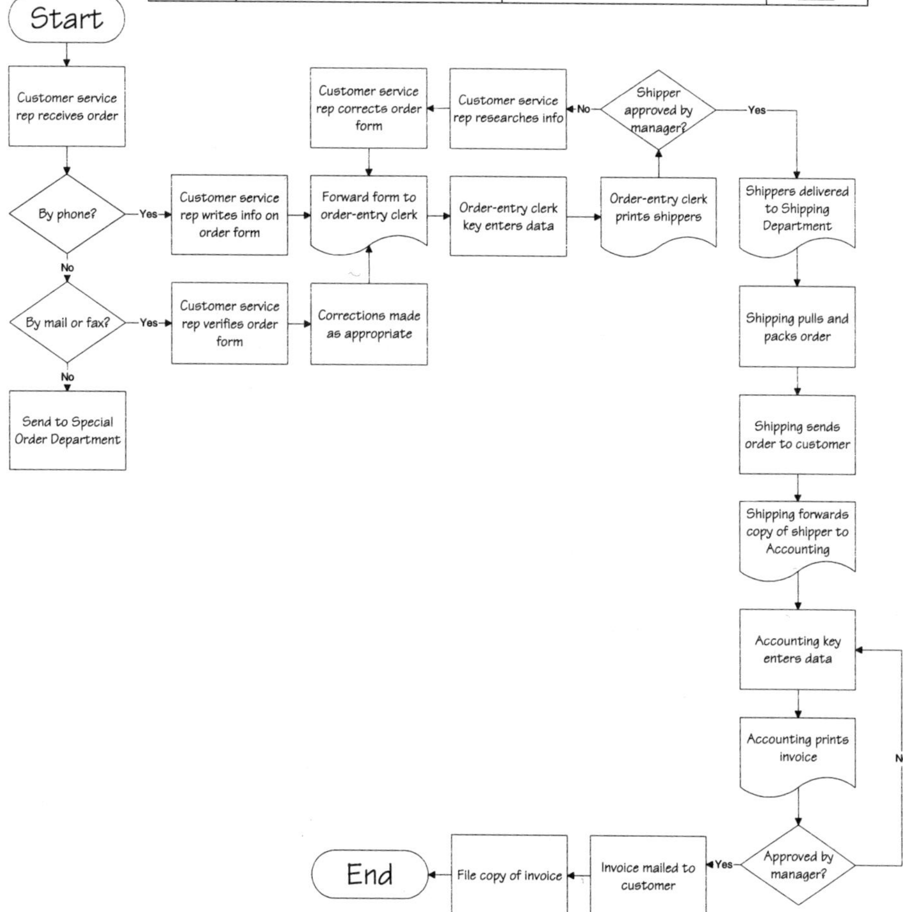

After you have documented the process, you're ready to measure it. Gathering performance data will show you where you need to improve. Or you may discover that the process isn't as deficient as you originally thought. Measurement clears up any discrepancies and provides an opportunity for comparison after your reengineered process has been implemented.

Look at each of the major process tasks on your list or flow chart and gather data for each necessary task or section of the process. The data you gather depends on what you wish to measure. Are you interested in the cost of the whole process? Or perhaps you want to measure the amount of time each task takes or how many approvals are necessary or how accurately some tasks are performed. Be sure to measure the *"as is"* capability of your current process in order to compare actual process performance to the *"new "* process requirements.

Shore Up's reengineering team...

looked at their *"new"* process requirements. *"Our customers want their merchandise shipped in a more timely manner,"* Mark said. *"So we need to determine just how long it takes us to ship."* Shelley snickered. *"I can make a good guess,"* she said. *"It takes about two weeks."* Mark turned to Joshua. *"Will you be willing to track all orders within the next two weeks and give us the average shipping time?"* Joshua nodded.

The team also looked at the other current and future customer requirements and decided to measure how long it took for customers to connect with service representatives and the percentage of problem resolutions.

The results gave the team a more accurate portrayal of what the current process was accomplishing. Joshua informed the team members that orders took an average of eight working days to reach the customer; five working days were required to fill the order at the facility. Customers also had to wait an average of two minutes before connecting with a representative, and 75% of problems were resolved upon first contact....

Envision Desired State

This part of the planning phase builds on your work accomplished in determining *"new"* process requirements, and takes it a step beyond. If everything is working as it should, what would things be like? You'll be looking at goals and desires.

Say your doctor has examined you and discovered that you're overweight and have out-of-sight cholesterol. She recommends that you change the way you eat and encourages you to start exercising. Your diet and exercise regimen *(or lack of it)* need major improvements. Your doctor has listed the results she wants you to accomplish *(e.g., reduce weight by fifteen pounds and cut cholesterol level from 280 to 200).* You even analyze your present way of eating *(whole milk, lots of fast-food high-fat items, plenty of sweets, etc.)* and your current amount of exercise *(walking to your garage, clicking the television's remote control, etc.).*

Now you have to imagine what you would like your new regimen *(process)* to consist of and what results you want to achieve. Maybe you'd like to lose twenty pounds and two inches around your waist. You envision yourself with a cholesterol level of 170, a smile on your face, clearer skin, and more energy. Your refrigerator is full of fruits and vegetables, and you even have a brand-new rowing machine.

Do the same envisioning with your process. Forget what the current process looks like, and focus on what the new process could be and what it could accomplish. And also look beyond the new process. Consider what the environment around the process should look like.

Ask yourself:

? How will the new process help the customer?

? How will it help the organization?

? How will the organizational environment change?

You may find it helpful to come up with a *"current limitations list"* that details all the factors that constrict your current process. List each on a separate piece of paper. Some of the items on your list may include:

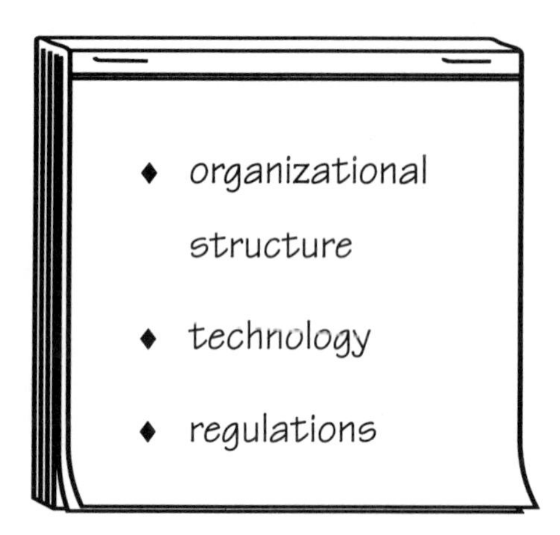

These factors may be limiting your process' potential. Draw a large "X" through each factor, hand one page *(or more than one, depending on the number of factors and number of individuals)* to each team member, and have the team members rip them up simultaneously. Now start to envision your new process, unencumbered by limitations.

This is your chance to dream. Maybe your customers want prices ten percent below what they are currently, but you envision a thirty-percent cut in manufacturing costs and would like to give them a twenty-percent reduction in product prices. Write that down. Perhaps your envisioning includes a zero-percent error rate or redesigning the physical placement of employees in your department. List it. Include any measures or factors you identified during benchmarking as being positive process characteristics. Brainstorm not only with your team members but also with employees of departments that will be impacted by the process-reengineering effort. Their insights will serve to enlarge the picture of your desired state. And they may address functions of the new process that you had not even considered.

Loudin suggested involving employees from many different departments in the envisioning step. So he met with representative groups from customer Service, Shipping, Order Entry, Finance, Catalogue Production, and Inventory planning at different times over a period of three weeks. He explained the process-reengineering effort, answered all questions, and encouraged their input.

He also asked them to envision themselves as customers of Shore Up in the year 2020. *"What's the interaction like between you and Shore Up?"* he asked. *"What's happening with the order-fulfillment process? How is it different?"*

The groups came up with a variety of goals and dreams for the new order-fulfillment process. Some of the goals and items that the team worked into their description of the *"desired state"* included:

- 100% customer satisfaction
- 100% resolution of customer problems on first contact
- Tracking of inventory by pen-sized scanners
- All orders shipped within 24 hours
- Special orders shipped within 48 hours
- No order forms—orders received by phone through voice recognition
- More "user-friendly" work areas (swivel chairs, headsets, larger computer screens, etc.)
- One or less approvals on all orders

Once you've envisioned your desired state, you have to return to reality and identify the difference between the current process and your ideal process.

Identify Process Performance *"Gaps"*

Completing this part of uncovering breakthrough improvements will clinch your decision of whether or not your process is one that should be reengineered. You'll use the data you gathered to measure the current process and compare it with your description of the ideal process. The difference between the two can be referred to as a process performance *"gap."* If the gap is slight, don't reengineer; consider continuous process improvement instead. But if the gap is great, prepare for a major effort.

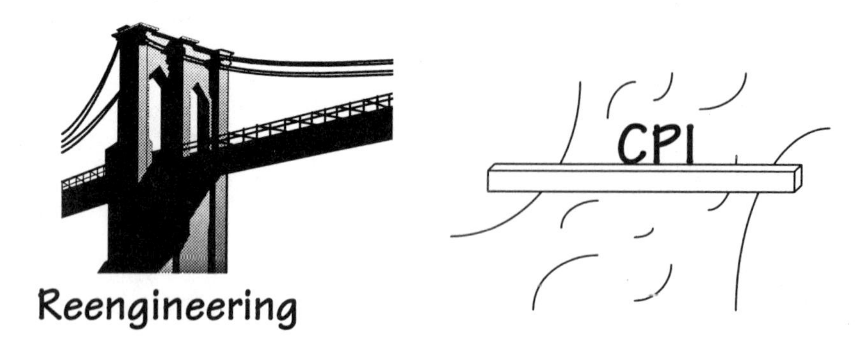

Also list the lessons you've learned from analyzing your *"as is"* process. Some proponents of process reengineering skip this activity. They'd rather you start from scratch and obliterate the old process from your memory. But that might not be to your advantage.

Some of the tasks in your process already work very well and may be more than appropriate for meeting all of the new customer requirements you've identified. You might want to include them *"as is"* in your reengineered process. Other tasks might be so detrimental to your organization that it's worthwhile remembering them so you don't design them into your new process.

Remember the health example in the previous step? Reengineering your regimen is in order, because you need to drop twenty pounds and lose that tire around your waist. A slight dose of improvement won't cut your cholesterol by eighty points. As for lessons learned from the old way of doing things, you know very well that if you stock your cupboards full of cookies, you'll succumb to the temptation and do away with dramatic improvement. So your new way of doing things will include stocking the cupboards with non-fattening treats.

If you brainstorm and list all the lessons you've learned from your old process, you'll increase your success rate with your new process.

Shore Up's process-reengineering team...

identified the process performance gaps. *"We have a 25% gap in problem resolution on first contact,"* Loudin began, *"and a gap of four working days in standard order fulfillment. In addition, we need to increase our customer satisfaction levels from 73% to 100%, and we need to update our technology. That's just the beginning."*

"I guess we'll be reengineering," Mark said. *"Which is what we thought we'd need to do."* *"Yes,"* Loudin responded, *"but now we know how far we have to go, and we can measure the improvements made by reengineering the order fulfillment process."*

The team continued their discussion by identifying more gaps and listing lessons learned from their present way of filling orders. *"We don't want to change the way the customer reps respond to customers,"* Shelley said. *"The customer surveys applauded my reps for being courteous. So we don't want to shortcut responses in an attempt to reach more customers quickly. Maybe we'll need to hire more reps or cross-train order-entry clerks."* *"Good observation,"* Loudin said. *"Any other lessons we've learned?"* The team started listing them.

Uncovering breakthrough opportunities is a challenging game. It provides you with the power to raise the stakes. If you're more sure than ever that process reengineering will work for your organization, head for the designing phase.

Chapter Five Worksheet: Is Reengineering In Your Organization's Future?

1. List the major tasks involved in your process.

2. Create a process flow chart that represents how your process currently flows.

3. Describe the results of your *"new process."* Envision it as a *"best-case scenario."* List how things will function 10 to 15 years in the future.

4. Briefly list any performance *"gaps"* that you can identify. *(Note: This will not be precise if you do not have current measurement data. If you do have that data, be specific in your identification of the gaps.)*

____

____

____

____

5. Is reengineering necessary to bridge those gaps or will process improvement cover them?

____

____

____

____

6. Are there any lessons you have learned from your current process *(i.e., did you do some things well or do you realize that you shouldn't do some things a certain way)?* If yes, briefly describe one such lesson learned.

____

____

____

____

MAP THE *"IDEAL"* PROCESS

Phase Two: Design Your Reengineered Process

Are you ready to get rid of the old process and design your new one? It will take perseverance, but the extra effort will result in a larger leap toward exceptional performance. Your job in this step of the designing phase, mapping the *"ideal"* process, is to do the legwork necessary for the leap. To map your *"ideal"* process, you must:

3. Map The "*Ideal*" Process
DESIGN
Phase Two D

1. Complete preliminary work
2. Set new goals and establish new measures, and
3. Create a new process flow chart

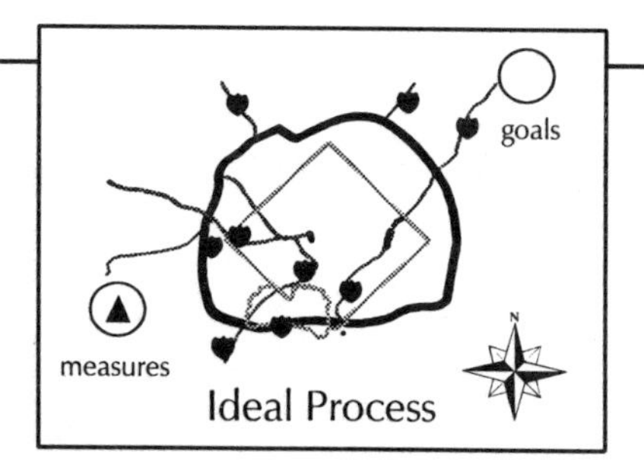

Complete Preliminary Work

You've identified process performance gaps in the previous step. Before you sit down to draw an actual map of the new process, you and your team must decide how you can close those gaps. How will you reduce manufacturing costs by 40%? Is it possible to cut cycle time in half? How do you eliminate numerous manager approvals and still maintain quality checks?

Maybe you've already decided upon a design that will achieve breakthrough opportunities. More than likely, however, you still have to consider the following *(which can take weeks)*:

Can we make the process simpler?

- Is our language or are our explanations too complex? Can we make them simpler?
- How about paperwork? Is there a way to simplify forms, reports, even memos?

Are we asking for unneeded reports or data?

- Are there any parts of the process that can be eliminated?

Can technology help?

- What tools or equipment can improve the process? How will they improve it?

Is new computer hardware or software necessary for our reengineering effort?

- Will we need to provide training for any new equipment?
- Do we need training to use already existing equipment?

Can we reduce time and/or cost?

- Where are the delays in our current process?
- Are steps designed in the correct order?
- Where are we getting the least amount of return?

These considerations, although general, apply to most organizations looking to improve processes. Don't attempt to reengineer a process unless you realize the existence and extent of your current process's deficiencies. Likewise, you also have to be aware of the opportunities available to you.

You can use the following *Process Design Alternatives Worksheet* to help you and your team think through your process.

Process Design Alternatives Worksheet

Key Task In Generic Terms	Current Process	Alternative Processes/Tasks
1. Get airline ticket for customer	Print ticket and mail to agent	Use electronic data to assign number to customer (no physical ticket)
2. ______________	______________	
3. ______________	______________	etc.
4.		

In the first column, list each key task of your process in generic terms, such as *"get airline ticket for customer."* In the second column, you will describe how that task is currently being completed *(e.g., print ticket and mail to agent, etc.)*. Question each word in the description and identify alternative tasks or processes *(e.g., fax ticket, use electronic data to assign number instead of producing ticket for customer, etc.)*.

Also encourage your team members to share their ideas and/or conclusions with employees who will be impacted by the reengineering effort. After all, they have a large stake in the effort. Your success is dependent upon them.

The team at Shore Up...,

spent a month looking for opportunities in reengineering their order-fulfillment process. Mark zeroed in on the order forms. *"First of all, they do need to be simplified for the customer. Then we can eliminate delays in trying to figure out what the customer really wants, which affects both our problem-resolution opportunity and our shipping time."* Shelley nodded. *"And redesigning the forms so they can be scanned will also reduce the amount of time it takes to read each form and enter it into the computer."*

Lonny, a customer-service rep whom Shelley asked to join the group, was particularly excited about the addition of software that would allow the reps to track inventory and the progress of a particular order. *"I really dislike telling a customer that I don't know whether we can fill their order or whether it's been shipped or is still sitting in a batch in the warehouse."* The team agreed, and each member confirmed and/or suggested ways to improve. Loudin asked the members to discuss the ideas with employees and return to the next meeting with additional input....

Set New Goals And Establish New Measures

Your preliminary work of figuring out how to bridge the gaps will come in handy for setting new goals and establishing new process measures. You may have decided that new computer software will help close one of your performance gaps, but it won't reach your ideal goal. That's okay. Sometimes you have to shoot for the stars to reach the treetops.

Set goals and establish measures worthy of your reengineering effort, but also be realistic. One-hundred percent customer satisfaction may only be achievable in a perfect world. Your best bet is to set goals and establish measures that at least meet customer requirements. From there, try to meet or beat what your competitors provide.

Loudin led the team in setting goals...

and establishing measures for the process being reengineered. *"Our customers are demanding faster shipment, and our competitors ship within twenty-four hours,"* Mark said. *"That needs to be one of our goals."*

"Well, what about our gap in problem resolution?" Shelley asked. *"I know the tracking capability will help in that instance, but are we really going to be able to resolve 100% of customer problems? I don't think so."* *"What if we set a goal of 92%?"* Joshua asked. *"Isn't that attainable?"*

"I think it could be," Loudin responded. *"After the reengineering, then, we may be able to identify areas of improvement dealing with just that problem and work on it from a standpoint of quality improvement."* The team continued listing their goals and measures....

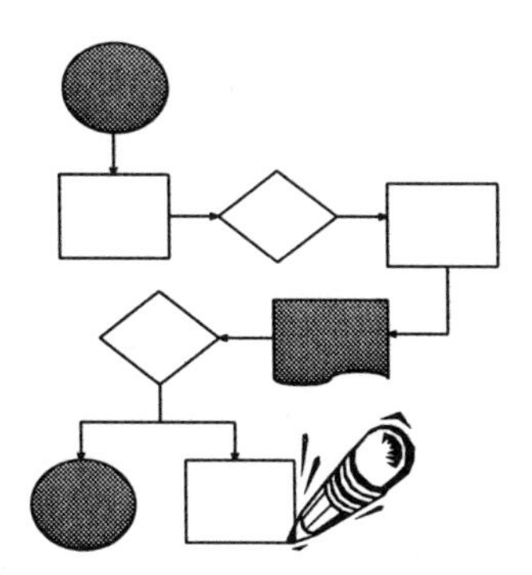

Create A New Process Flow Chart

Start with a blank slate and work on designing a flow chart for your new process. Reengineering involves more than pinning up your old flow chart and tearing off chunks of it. Reengineering a process means that you are doing something new, not just reducing the old.

Creating a new process flow chart takes time. You and your team may come up with what you consider a fantastic chart, only to have a manager of a certain department tell you it's not feasible. That's why it is best to solicit input from various departments and employees when you're considering how to bridge the performance gaps. Always check each section of the process with the employees working directly with *(or with the "owners" of)* the process after you've finished flow charting it.

If you remember these three steps—

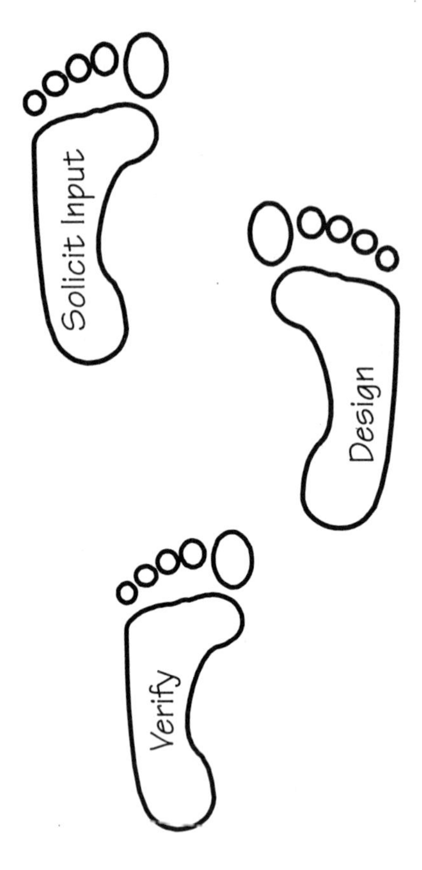

you will encompass more possibilities and eliminate more uncertainties in your new process flow chart.

The process-reengineering team...

spent days working through the logistics of the new process flow chart. They worked on the process from input to output, and checked with employees and managers alike to verify the possibilities. The flow chart they finally decided upon looked quite different from the flow chart depicting their original order-fulfillment process. Here is a sample of the new flow chart:

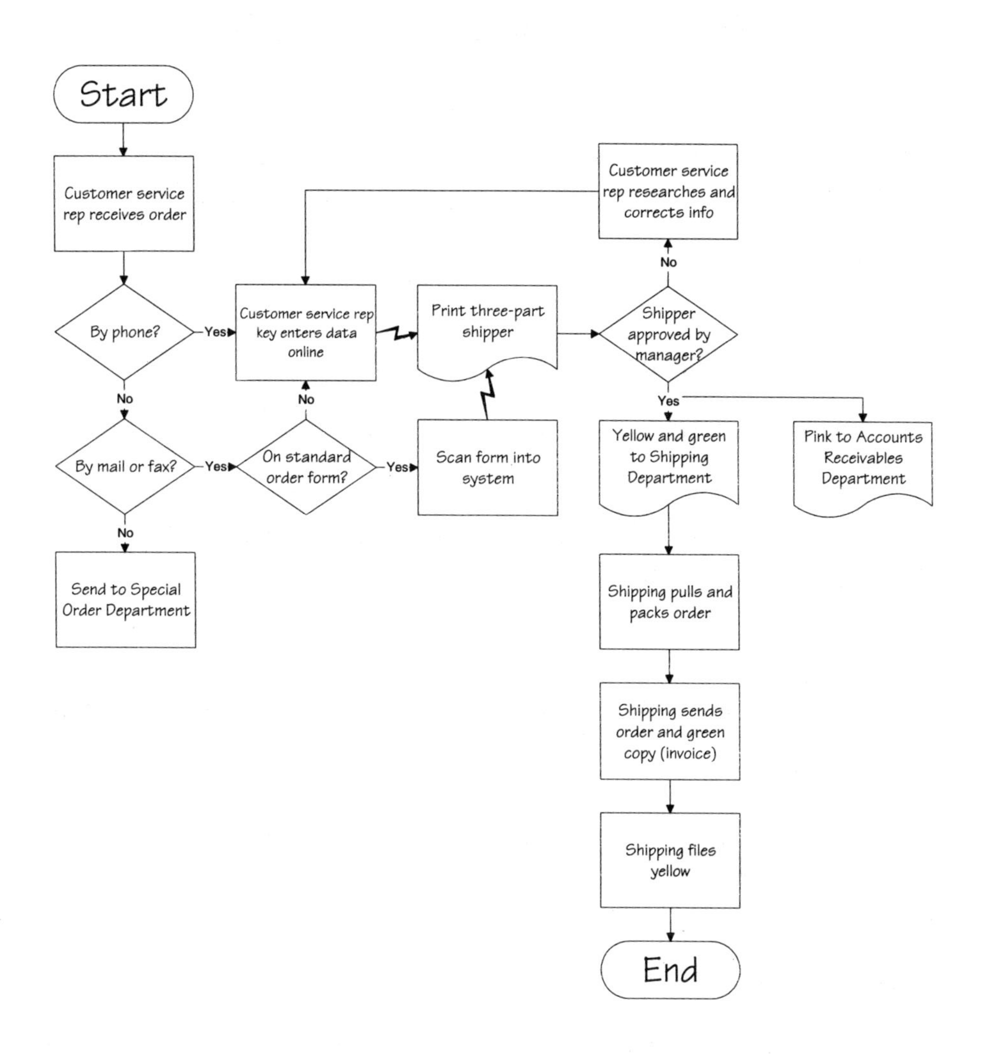

Mapping the *"ideal"* process results in a practical application of your planning effort. You're over the initial hump of work. Next, you will work on redefining your process support requirements.

CHAPTER SIX WORKSHEET: COMPLETING YOUR PRELIMINARY WORK

1. Think carefully about your reengineering effort. Then look over each of the following major questions and preliminary considerations. Place a checkmark by each question that applies to your situation.

_____ **Can We Make The Process Simpler?**

- Is our language or are our explanations too complex? Can we make them simpler?
- How about paperwork? Is there a way to simplify forms, reports, even memos?
- Are we asking for unneeded reports or data?
- Are there any parts of the process that can be eliminated?

_____ **Can Technology Help?**

- What tools or equipment can improve the process? How will they improve?
- Is new computer hardware or software necessary for our reengineering effort?
- Will we need to provide training for any new equipment?
- Do we need training to use already existing equipment?

_____ **Can We Reduce Time And/Or Cost?**

- Where are the delays in our current process?
- Are steps designed in the correct order?
- Where are we getting the least amount of return?

2. Choose one of the questions by which you placed a checkmark, answer it, and briefly describe how you will respond for your reengineering effort.

____

____

____

____

____

____

____

3. Develop a response for each of the other questions you have marked in Question # 1.

____

____

____

____

____

____

____

REDEFINE PROCESS SUPPORT REQUIREMENTS

Phase Two D
4. Redefine Process Support Requirements
DESIGN

You've mapped your *"new"* process by creating a flow chart that identifies the steps in your process, and you've established new measures for the process. Now you have to decide what your new process requires to support it. Will you need to redesign jobs? Maybe a new computer system is in your future. Or perhaps you've discovered you need to create new forms to track information. What will it take for your reengineered process to operate as designed?

You'll be looking at three different areas of support within an organization that need to be redefined whenever you reengineer a process:

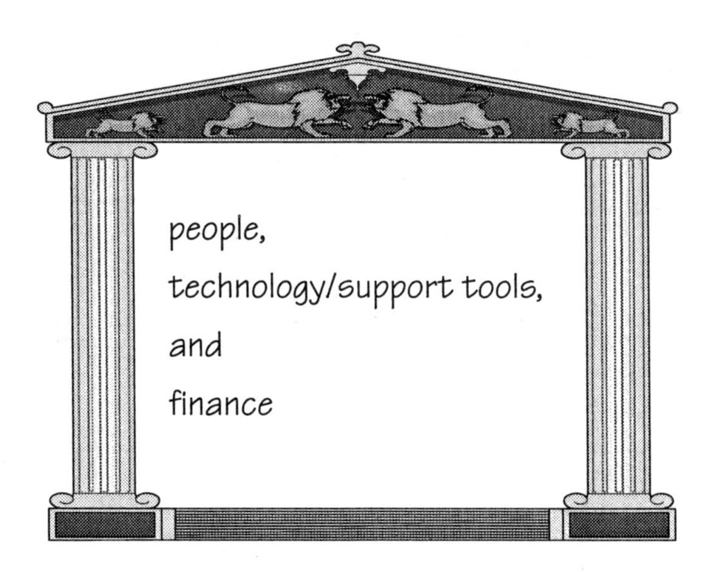

What Will You Require Of The People In Your Organization?

Process reengineering includes a human element. If your process is completed by people, they will be impacted by the reengineering effort. After all, you may have to redesign the way they do a portion of their jobs, eliminate some of their work, or even totally change what they are required to do.

Part of designing a reengineered process involves discovering how it changes the work people do. Maybe one of your requirements is that everyone in the finance department learns how to use the new budgeting software. Or perhaps you'll no longer have your organization divided into departments; instead, you'll organize work around cross-functional teams and/or *"core"* processes.

You might want to fill out a *Role-Transition Worksheet* for each position that will change when your reengineered process takes effect. You'll list the present and future job responsibilities. That will give you a handle on new job requirements.

ROLE-TRANSITION WORKSHEET			
POSITION TITLE:		FUTURE TITLE:	
PRESENT RESPONSIBILITIES		FUTURE RESPONSIBILITIES	
KEY FUNCTIONS	KEY RESPONSIBILITIES	ADDITIONS (*) DELETIONS (-)	TARGETED RESULTS

Loudin led the reengineering team...

in brainstorming the changes the new process would require of the employees at Shore Up. The team began by identifying the new requirements for order-entry clerks and customer-service representatives. *"Didn't we decide that we were going to train the two groups?"* Shelley asked.

"I think that's the best solution," Mark said. *"Since we'll have scannable forms for the mail orders, order-entry clerks will deal only with phone orders. And since one of our goals is to respond more quickly to our customers, having clerks and reps that can do both jobs will eliminate some waiting time. They can all be called customer representatives and will need to learn the new computer software for entering and accessing data for tracking customer orders."*

The team filled out a Role-Transition Worksheet for the clerks and representatives to clarify the new responsibilities of all customer representatives. Following is a sample of their worksheet....

ROLE-TRANSITION WORKSHEET			
POSITION TITLE:	Order Clerk & Customer Service Rep	FUTURE TITLE:	Customer Rep
PRESENT RESPONSIBILITIES		FUTURE RESPONSIBILITIES	
KEY FUNCTIONS	KEY RESPONSIBILITIES	ADDITIONS (*) DELETIONS (-)	TARGETED RESULTS
Service Customers	Resolve problems	*Key in orders, payment	Check for 100% accuracy
	Answer questions	*Track inventory	Provide immediate feedback on in-stock items
	Provide product information	*Follow-up on every order	Meet delivery time of 24 hours

What Technology/Support Tools Will You Require?

Today's organizations have a better chance of succeeding in making breakthrough improvements than organizations of previous decades, because of the potential of today's technologies for controlling work, imparting mastery, communicating, and accessing information by employees, customers, and suppliers.

Technology can be as complicated and/or costly as a state-of-the-art computer system and software that serves one-thousand employees, or it can be as simple and inexpensive as purchasing a fax machine to process requests and send price quotes more efficiently. If you have identified a technological tool that will support your reengineered process, factor it into your design.

Benchmarking can be especially helpful here. If other organizations are using technology to meet customer demands, you might decide to follow suit. Maybe you never envisioned using electric conveyor belts at your facility, but a competitor benefits greatly from them. Perhaps another company utilizes a centralized 1-800 number to generate consumer interest, and it works for them. Such technology may help your organization.

If technology can reduce the amount of time or trouble it takes to reach your ideal state, consider it an important process support requirement. But do not rely on it alone. For example, suppose a manufacturing company wants to make more tennis shoes to meet customer demands. So they purchase new machinery that cuts manufacturing time by a third. But the shoes sit in boxes, because they forgot to redesign the packaging and shipping process.

Technology is often an essential ingredient of process reengineering, but it takes more support to create a recipe for success. Decide whether technology is a must for your reengineered process, and choose the type of technology that is needed.

While technology support can be considered a tool, its companion category of support tools includes other items, such as office furniture, new forms, additional telephones, etc. Process reengineering often demands such support that may not appear essential, but in reality, is definitely necessary.

Look at the flow chart of your new process. Do you need to redesign any of your current forms, catalogs, or training manuals? List them. Will you need to hire more people, all of whom require additional office space and desks, chairs, phones, and personal computers?

You might require additional workspace for your reengineered process. Don't neglect to include it. Or what about a new electric panel? A new sign? If your reengineered process demands it, you're under obligation to list it. Otherwise, you might stall the reengineering effort.

Talk to the employees who will be affected by the reengineered process. What will they need? If they realize that you are open to their concerns and opinions, your implementation will go much smoother, and your support requirements will be more complete.

The reengineering team...

at Shore Up spent a few weeks questioning employees and themselves about the technological and support tools that were critical to their reengineering of the order fulfillment process. Loudin summarized their technological needs. *"We have to purchase a new computer system and software that will allow us to track inventory. We also need to buy scanners to scan the new order forms. As far as technology is concerned, those are our basic requirements."*

"But our list of support tools is much longer," Mark added. *"We're going to need more telephones, and we have to purchase headsets for customer reps. Then we need redesigned desks with swivel chairs."* Shelley joined in. *"The reps are asking for cubicles that are more soundproof,"* she said.

"And the order-entry clerks, or I should say the future customer representatives, would like any items that will help eliminate computer fatigue," Joshua added. *"They'd like reduced-glare screens, a more user-friendly mouse, and more deluxe wrist rests." "What about new forms that can be scanned?"* Lonny brought up. *"Don't we have to design those?"* The team continued discussing the support requirements....

What Financial Support Does Your Reengineered Process Require?

Wouldn't it be great if you could go ahead with your reengineering plan without having to consider its cost? Well, you could, but the results might prove disastrous. You want your reengineering effort to have a positive impact on your organization. You don't want to achieve marked improvement if it will ruin your organization financially.

Remember the car wash reengineering project? That team was able to redesign the process so cars could be washed more quickly, but it cost them money in additional labor. However, if the new speed with which they washed cars attracted more customers, the reengineered process would be an unqualified success.

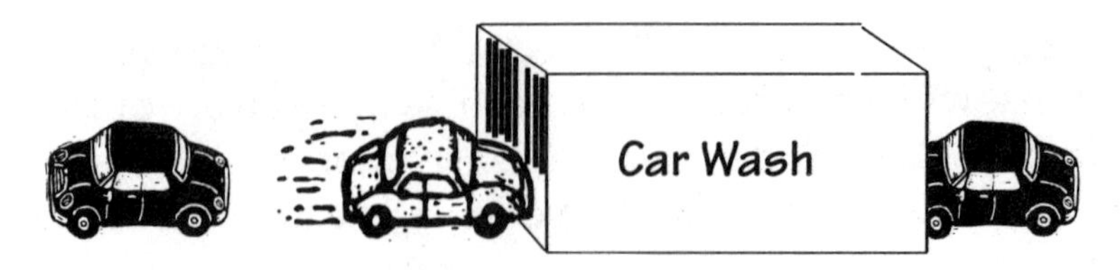

You will have to conduct a cost/benefit analysis of your reengineering project to determine whether it's advisable to move forward. Cost/benefit analysis can be described as:

> A complete, realistic comparison of costs and resulting benefits associated with implementing a decision.

If you're contemplating whether to recommend continuing with the reengineering effort, you're probably weighing a number of cost/benefit considerations:

- What are the "*current*" and "*desired*" states and their corresponding measures?
- What are the realistic costs related to reengineering?
- What tangible and intangible benefits will result from the reengineering effort, both long- and short-term?
- Which benefits are most important to customers?
- How will we ultimately balance the cost and benefit factors to make a decision?

Analyzing cost/benefit data can become a complicated process, but you can use several techniques to simplify your efforts. One tip is to list all costs and benefits related to an improvement option in two or three major categories or "buckets."

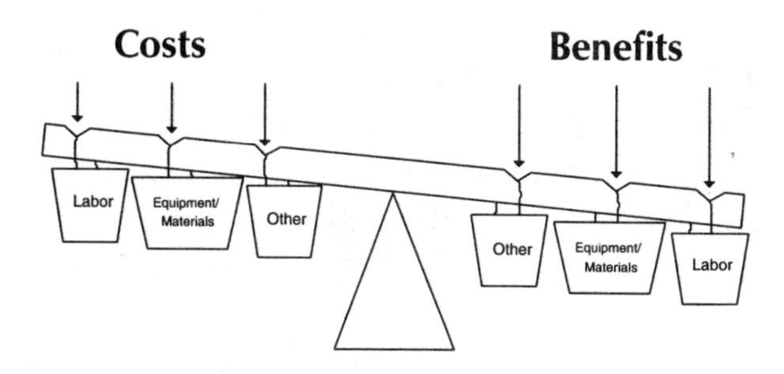

Some of the potential *"line items"* you may want to identify within these categories include:

COSTS (*Measurable Outlays*)	BENEFITS (*Increases/Decreases*)
Labor: • Salaries • Benefits • Training • Contractor/consultant fees	**Labor:** • Productivity • Absenteeism • Contractor/consultant fees • Cycle time • Timeliness • Safety • Turnover • New skills • Accuracy • Reassignment • Permanent versus temp • Staffing
Equipment/Materials: • Information hardware/software • Tools/machinery • Furniture • Supplies • Data	**Equipment/Materials:** • Downtime • Efficiency/performance • Cycle time • Accuracy • Quality • Amount required • Set-up
Other: • Downtime (*in terms of delivery to customer*) • Less tangible items (*morale, complaints, etc.*)	**Other:** • Customer-related improvements • Product quality • Service quality • Functional/departmental measures • Less tangible items

Determine the cost/benefit categories for your organization; then gather the data for each *("guesstimating" when necessary)* and calculate the cost/benefit relationship. Check out the Cost/Benefit Model in the Appendix for more detailed information on these steps.

The reengineering team had their work... cut out for them. Mark asked the Chief Financial Officer, Victoria, to join the team. *"We can use your expertise,"* he told her. Then he assigned each team member to research and come up with estimated costs and benefits for the various categories. A week later, they met and discussed their results. A sample of their cost/benefit calculation worksheet follows:

Cost/Benefit Calculation Worksheet

Scenario: ☐ Best ☑ Probable ☐ Worst
All figures are: ☑ Annual ☐ Monthly ☐ Other________

Costs

Category/ Process Factor	Amount	Total
Labor Category		
Ongoing		
Computer maintenance	$1,200	
Salary for trainer & trainees	$42,000	
Benefits (25%)	$10,500	
Training updates/re-fresher	$500	
One-time		
Programming consultant	$2,000	
Train current staff on new software	$1,700	
Equipment/Materials Category		
Ongoing		
N/A		
One-time		
Computer hardware	$5,000	
Computer software	$2,100	
Scanners	$14,500	
Redesign of order forms	$5,000	
Other Categories		
Ongoing		
Overhead allocation ($125/mo.)	$1,500	
One-time		
N/A		
Totals Ongoing:		$55,700
One-time:		$30,300
Total:		$86,000

Benefits

Category/ Process Factor	Amount	Total
Labor Category		
Ongoing		
Reduction in need to hire additional order-entry clerks and customer service reps		$89,030
One-time		
N/A		
Equipment/Materials Category		
Ongoing		
N/A		
One-time		
N/A		
Other Categories		
Ongoing		
Return phone calls to customers		$200
Savings from reduced order duplication		$1,200
One-time		
N/A		
Totals Ongoing:		$90,430
One-time:		$Ø
Total:		$90,430

Comparison Of Costs And Benefits

	Year 1 (*One-time + Ongoing*)	Year 2+ (*Ongoing*)
Total Benefits =	$ 90,430	$ 90,430
Total Costs =	$ 86,000	$ 55,700
Difference ($Benefits – $Costs)=	$ + 4,430	$ + 34,760

(If the difference is positive, the option being considered may be a viable one; however, the magnitude of the difference should be examined. See the section below.)

Magnitude Of Difference

ROI = Return On Investment = $\frac{\textit{return} - \textit{investment}}{\textit{investment}}$ X 100=_______ %

Where: ***return***=*benefits – ongoing costs*
investment=*one-time costs*

By End Of Year 1

ROI = $\frac{\textit{return} - \textit{investment}}{\textit{investment}}$ X 100=

$$\frac{(90{,}430 - 55{,}700) - 30{,}300}{30{,}300} \times 100$$

$$= \frac{4{,}430}{30{,}300} \times 100$$

$$= 14.6\%$$

By End Of Year 2

$$\frac{(180{,}860 - 111{,}400) - 30{,}300}{30{,}300} \times 100$$

$$= \frac{39{,}160}{30{,}300} \times 100$$

$$= 129.2\%$$

Conclusion(s)/Recommendation(s)

1. By the end of Year 1 the proposal has earned a modest but respectable ROI.
2. By the end of Year 2 the proposal shows a substantial positive ROI.
3. One risk: reengineered process may be copied by competitors.
4. Recommendation—implement the proposal, seek a very creative staff member.

Their conclusions looked promising. *"This reengineering effort is not inexpensive,"* Loudin began, *"but it appears that the results in customer satisfaction and repeat purchases will offset the costs. Besides,"* he added, *"the cost of not reengineering is prohibitive. So let's keep going."*

By redefining your process support requirements, you have a greater knowledge of what reengineering your process entails. If the benefits appropriately outweigh the costs, you have the green light to begin developing your change management plan.

Chapter Seven Worksheet: Determining Your Process Support Requirements

1. What jobs will be impacted by your reengineering effort? List them.

____

____

____

____

2. List any technology and/or support tools that you'll need for your reengineered process.

____

____

____

____

____

3. For one of the jobs you listed, fill out a photocopy of a blank *Role-Transition Worksheet* included in the Appendix.

4. Using a photocopy of the blank *Cost/Benefit Worksheet* included in the Appendix, complete a cost/benefit analysis of your reengineering effort.

Develop Change Management Plan

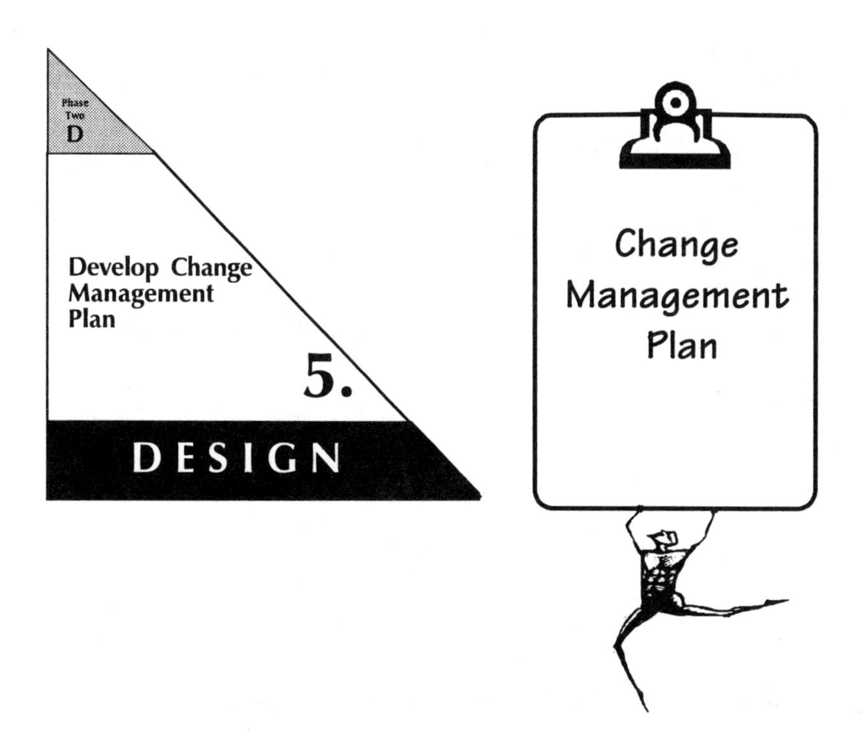

You're getting closer to making the quantum leap toward radical improvement. In this last step of the Designing Phase, you'll be developing a change-management plan that will help your organization execute the leap as flawlessly as possible.

Consider Organizational Impact

You've redefined the process support requirements. Now you need to analyze the impact of your reengineered process. Too many organizations neglect this important step, because they feel analysis is a waste of time. It is not. Analyzing the impact is critical if you desire your new process to radically change the way your organization operates.

Consider the following:

- Who and what will be impacted, and how?
- What emotional factors need to be incorporated into the change management plan?
- How will the plan be monitored?
- Have all those who will be affected by the reengineered process been consulted about potential impact?
- Will the plan be designed to foster involvement and commitment to the recommended changes?

Who and what will be impacted, and how?

Your team has already identified the tasks and organizational factors that will be affected by your reengineered process. And hopefully, you have already been informing and soliciting information from the employees who will be affected by the new process.

Now you need to take a closer look at the specific impacts. Go beyond what you did in the previous chapter in redefining process support requirements. Write new job descriptions for those whose jobs will change. Draw out the new organizational structure and write a new mission statement, or list your organization's new values. If management practices will change, describe them in writing.

Next, take a good look at the employees who will be affected, and determine the extent of impact. Process reengineering involves radical change; your effort may affect more people than you imagine. List all those whose work processes, work style, attitudes, etc. will have to change along with the reengineered process. In many cases, your list may include the entire organization. Decide how the employees will be impacted by the changes ahead.

What emotional factors need to be incorporated into your change management plan?

Emotions will run high whenever a change is in progress. When the change involves process reengineering, emotions may become uncontrollable. That is why your team will have to incorporate into your plan some way to manage emotions. If you do, you won't be taken by surprise when they surface *(which they definitely will).*

Consider ways to manage:

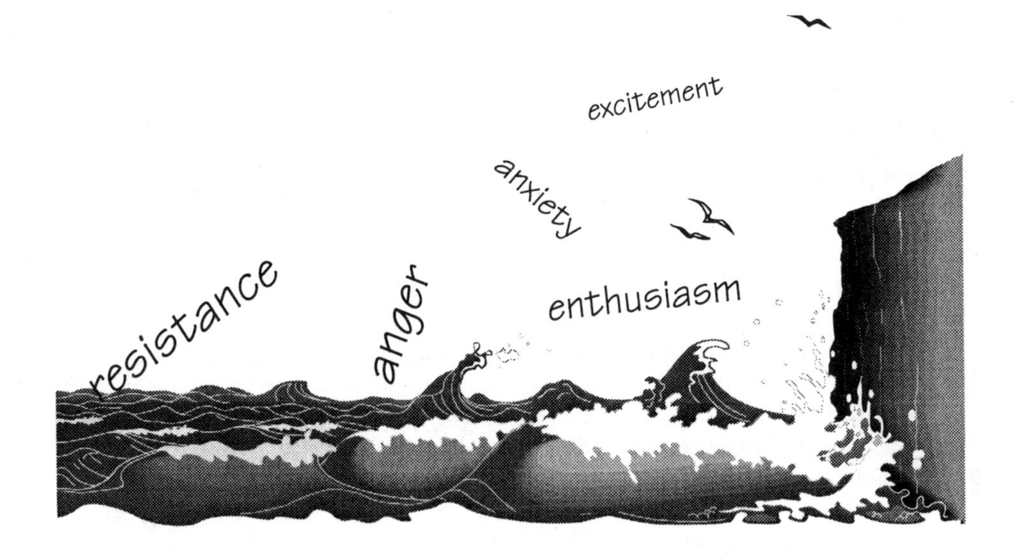

For more information on how you can manage negative reactions to your effort, read *Mastering Change Management*, one of the guidebooks in the Management Skills Series.

How will the change management plan be monitored?

For your reengineering effort to reach its goal of unprecedented improvement, you will have to monitor it effectively. Considerations include:

- Who will direct your change management plan?
- Who should be involved in identifying and resolving key issues?
- What kind of tracking system will you use?
- What methods will you use to incorporate additional points into your plan?

Clarify these points up front, and you will save headaches down the line.

The reengineering team at Shore Up...

decided that Mark and Loudin would direct the plan. *"Since reengineering is such a dramatic change, direction needs to come from the top,"* Loudin said. *"Besides, any one manager doesn't have the authority or the vision to make some of the cross-functional decisions that reengineering demands."* The team, however, would be responsible for identifying and resolving any key issues. As for tracking, they began working on ways they could measure all the changes ahead. The new computer software would track the timeliness of each order, and Shelley had devised a form to track problem resolution. Joshua was in charge of overseeing the success of the new scanning process, and Loudin was working on a new customer satisfaction survey....

Have all those affected by the reengineered process been consulted about potential impact?

Your team has been doing this all along, as well it should. This issue needs to be dealt with continually. At every step in each phase, you need to consult those who will be impacted by the reengineered process. Even after the changes are implemented, this issue will still be important.

You may have discovered that the effort will affect many more employees than you originally thought. Get them involved in the effort now! Ask for their input and see to it that you use it to your advantage.

> ***Shore Up's reengineering team...***
> did uncover more employees who would be affected by the new process. *"I really didn't think those in finance would be affected on a daily basis by the new order-fulfillment process,"* Victoria offered, *"but they will be. Since orders have to be handled much more quickly, that means that checks have to be verified immediately. Approvals can't wait in the in-baskets for days." "Start talking to your employees right away,"* Loudin suggested. *"They need to be in on the reengineering effort, too."*

Will the change management plan foster involvement and commitment to the recommended changes?

If your organization's employees are committed to the reengineering effort, your ability to make a radical change is enhanced. Help all those affected by the change to keep the *"greater"* goal foremost in their minds.

In some cases, this means articulating the *"greater"* goal. You should have already been communicating your intent. If you haven't, your team needs to formulate a case for the reengineered process.

Include:

- Why is the process being reengineered? *(Let them know the driving forces behind your effort—customer needs, competitive advantage, etc. If your organization would fold without this last-ditch attempt, say so. Knowing their jobs would be in jeopardy without this move can be a great incentive to support it.)*

- What are the benefits? *(Will customers flock to your organization? Will company stock, which they have an interest in, rise as a result? Maybe they will be given more decision-making opportunities, as the layers of the organization are stripped away. They may learn new skills, which will increase their opportunities. It could even be that the whole atmosphere or environment will be more conducive to their input.)*

- Are there any employee concerns that need to be addressed? *(Think about what fears they may harbor. Do they feel they will have to work much harder or put in longer hours? Are they afraid they will lose their jobs? Maybe they are afraid some of their power will be taken away. Answer each concern as honestly as possible. Don't minimize risks but do focus on the benefits.)*

Design Your Change Management Plan

This is the final segment of the designing phase. You and your reengineering team have mapped your *"ideal"* process, redefined your process support requirements, and analyzed organizational impact. You'll complete Phase Two by designing your change management plan. Do so by:

- Identifying change management plan requirements
- Choosing a planning process and format, and
- Deciding how to move the Action Plan forward

Identifying change management plan requirements

Identifying action-plan requirements builds on the requirements you've set for the new process. You now need to decide what you will need to get you from the old process to the new one. What will it take?

- Time?
- Money?
- Acting managers?
- Consultants?
- New roles?
- Etc.?

This is not a repeat of determining your new process requirements, although it may overlap at times. You have to decide what the change management plan will require. Will you need to hire temporary help while you train employees? Will consultants be in charge of training? How much time will it take to complete each step of your plan? Will you need to form new teams to choose the best machinery or computer system for your organization? Consider all your requirements.

The process-reengineering team...

at Shore Up began listing the requirements of their change management plan on a flip chart. *"Training is going to be a major portion of our plan,"* Loudin said. *"And I think you might want to consider hiring consultants to develop a training program to help customer representatives use the new software we decide to purchase. We don't have the time." "Good point,"* Mark responded, *"because we still have to re-train the shipping department to fill orders immediately, and the accountants have to learn the new procedure for check approvals."*

"Who's going to produce the new catalog?" Shelley asked. *"And do we know what scanner we'll purchase or what desks? There are a lot of considerations here." "You're absolutely right,"* Loudin said, as he continued to list the requirements on the flip chart. . . .

REQUIREMENTS

- Consultants
- Catalog
- Scanner

Choosing a planning process and format

Listing the requirements is not enough. Your team will need to devise an Action Plan that is both detailed and specific. Whatever process and format you choose to use, make sure it includes all major activities and then details specific responsibilities.

Shore Up's reengineering team...

decided to fill out a Task/Responsibility Matrix to help them identify various tasks and assign responsibility to each. They began by identifying tasks related to the training of the new customer representatives. They decided which team members or outside consultants would be responsible for the tasks. For each task, a *"P"* was assigned to represent a primary responsibility, and *"S"* if it was a secondary responsibility, a *"C"* if the person or group needed to be in the communication loop, a *"+"* if the rating demanded extra emphasis, and it was left blank if there was no relationship between an individual or a group and the task.

Take a look at one portion of the reengineering team's Task/Responsibility Matrix:

TASK/RESPONSIBILITY MATRIX							
	RESPONSIBILITY						
TASK	Mark	Loudin	Shelley	Joshua	Victoria	Lonny	Consultants
Choose and purchase new software	P	C	S	S	C		
Design training program	C	C	C	C			P
Conduct training	C	C	P	S+		C	

P = Primary responsibility **S**= Secondary responsibility **C**= Communication loop

Loudin asked the team members to return to the next meeting with a more detailed plan and an idea of the cost for each task for which they were responsible. . . .

It doesn't matter what format you use for your Action Plan, as long as it includes project timetables. And to best ensure a nearly flawless execution of your specific plan, you should consider contingency plans, feedback, and communication systems.

At the team's next meeting...

Loudin immediately involved the team members in creating an Action Plan for implementing the changes. Their action plan was an extension of their Task/Responsibility Matrix. Along with the task and responsible person and/or group, it included the projected dates, an estimation of the hours involved, and the cost.

Here is a portion of the reengineering team's Action Plan for implementing the changes:

ACTION PLAN					
ACTION STEP/ TASK	RESPONSIBLE PERSON/TEAM	BEGIN DATE	END DATE	EST. HOURS	EST. COST
Choose and purchase new software	Mark (P) Shelley Joshua	5/10	5/17	15	
Design training program	Outside consultants	5/20	6/10	200	$8,000
Conduct training	Shelley (P) Joshua	6/15	7/31	20-40	$600-$1,200

The contingency plans you decide upon will enable you to cover your bases if something unexpected occurs during implementation, or if you are too pressed for time to finish your task. You might, for example, choose to hire consultants to train your employees if you don't have the expertise or time. Or you might ask one of the organizations you benchmarked to recommend their choice of software if, again, the group tasked with that decision doesn't have the know-how or the time.

Deciding how to move the Action Plan forward

You already realize your Action Plan will impact a number of your organization's employees. If you have planned sufficiently, they are aware of the process-reengineering effort, have provided valuable input, and are willing participants. Let them in on your plan.

Factor in how you'll kick off the reengineering effort, get progress updates, and keep employees excited about the changes. If these concerns are designed into your Action Plan, implementing the changes will be much easier.

Make sure:

- Proper attention is given to roles, responsibilities, structures, and resources
- Change effort is made a top priority
- Needed resource people are freed up from their normal responsibilities
- Implementation timetable is realistic

Developing a change management plan for your reengineered process wraps up the designing phase. You are now prepared for the implementation work ahead. Keep up the good work!

Chapter Eight Worksheet: Producing Your Action Plan

1. List all the people and areas that will be impacted by your process-reengineering effort, and explain how.

____

____

____

2. Check the emotions you expect from employees during implementation of the new process.

_____ Excitement

_____ Enthusiasm

_____ Disbelief

_____ Anger

_____ Resistance

_____ Anxiety

_____ Other *(please list)* ______________________

3. Describe how you will monitor your change management plans.

____

____

____

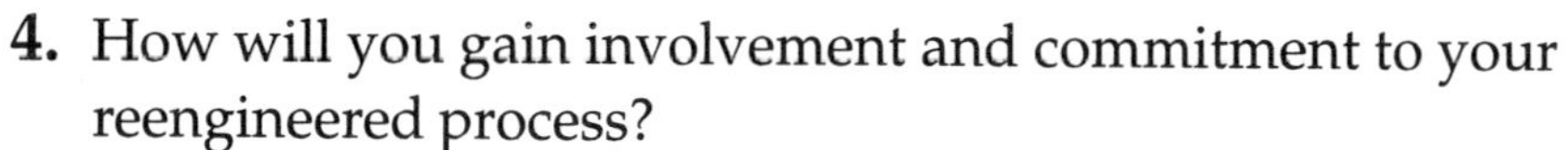

4. How will you gain involvement and commitment to your reengineered process?

____

____

____

5. Complete a detailed Action Plan for at least one change in your process-reengineering effort. Be sure to include tasks, person(s) responsible, timetables, estimated hours, and estimated cost.

ACTION PLAN					
ACTION STEP/ TASK	RESPONSIBLE PERSON/TEAM	BEGIN DATE	END DATE	EST. HOURS	EST. COST

Phase Three: Implement Your Reengineered Process

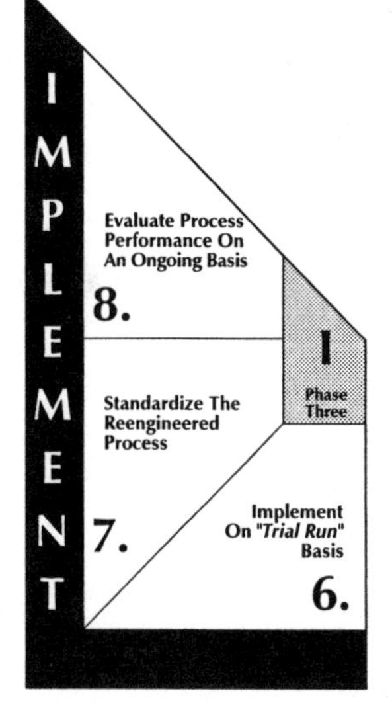

You're nearing the countdown, when the intense effort you and your team have expended on reengineering your process will come to fruition. Process reengineering is both complex and time-consuming. Yet the rewards can be tremendous. This final phase in the Process-Reengineering Model consists of three steps:

- Implement on "trial run" basis
- Standardize the reengineered process
- Evaluate process performance on an ongoing basis

Implement On *"Trial Run"* Basis

You're at the edge of the cliff, ready to make the leap that will vault you over the abyss of mediocrity. But wait: don't you think it would be beneficial to take a trial leap, just to ensure that your final jump won't end in disaster? It's similar to taking a driving test before you're allowed to drive unsupervised on the road. Your *"trial run"* will determine if you should receive your license to proceed with your process-reengineering effort.

It's not an easy task to implement your reengineered process on a trial-run basis. And it could very well take up to six months. But it is a vital step in the implementation phase.

Conduct a pilot test

Conduct a thorough pilot test before moving into full implementation. This will ensure that the proposed changes will dramatically improve the process. It will also reveal unanticipated problems and help build acceptance, support, and enthusiasm for the reengineered process before it is implemented on a full-scale basis.

Conducting a pilot test to assess your recommended changes will take some ingenuity on your team's part. Your organization's reengineering effort may be vastly different from that of another, so it is difficult to suggest any one way to handle the pilot test. You will have to analyze the scope of your effort and the resources and time available.

Perhaps your organization's process-reengineering effort will affect five hundred franchises across the country. You might choose to conduct a pilot test in five of those franchises. Or maybe your effort involves changes to a number of departments within your organization. You may opt to test your changes within only one department or one at a time until all changes have been tested. It's your call.

Assess the results and make necessary adjustments

Once you've conducted a pilot test, determine whether it was successful. Gather data on the new process measures you set in the designing phase and determine if the changes will meet your goals.

Your measures may include some of the following:

- Number of customer complaints, responses, calls
- Number of errors and corrections
- Frequency and volume of transactions
- Timing of tasks or process
- Number of employees required to complete the process
- Customer satisfaction

Your pilot test should indicate whether your process-reengineering effort gets a green light to continue moving ahead. Maybe your results of the pilot test indicate a yellow light—proceed with caution. You might need to make some minor adjustments to your flow chart. Or your pilot test might have flashed a red light. If that's the case, return to the beginning of the designing phase and retrace your steps.

Shore Up's process-reengineering team...
decided to conduct a pilot test by implementing some of the changes that would affect timely delivery of their merchandise. The company purchased the new computer system and software, and Joshua and Shelley learned how to use it. They were slated to train all the customer representatives during full implementation of the effort.

In addition, employees in Shipping/Warehouse were instructed in the new procedures, and so were those in Accounting. The pilot test went fairly well. The process-reengineering team identified some quirks in the shipping process, but it didn't take long to amend those. And by the end of one week, most orders were shipped within twenty-four hours. *"Holiday times will prove to be the real test,"* Loudin said. *"But I think we're ready to start implementing."*...

If the data you gather from your pilot test support that a real change has occurred, you are on the right track. But more important, you should discover whether the customer notices a difference. Does the data reflect what the customer really desires? If your answer is an unqualified *"yes,"* forge ahead.

Standardize The Reengineered Process

Once your pilot test reveals you are ready to implement your reengineered process, set your Action Plan in motion. You may have completed some of the tasks in your plan during the pilot test; continue where you left off until all the tasks are finished. Then your task becomes one of standardizing the reengineered process.

Standardizing means that you desire your new process to become an accepted and established process within your organization. You might document the new process and write down the new guidelines. You could publish those guidelines in a company newsletter and/or communicate them in group meetings.

You will also revise any of the new job descriptions you wrote so that they accurately reflect the new process. Include new expectations in the descriptions. And be sure to distribute copies of the descriptions to the employees.

Your success in standardizing the new process will depend in part on how much employee *"buy-in"* you have. If you sought after buy-in from the beginning, this step will be easier. Encourage employee participation and stay focused on the customer. Share customer-survey data with all employees and keep your process-reengineering effort aimed directly at the customer.

Evaluate Process Performance On An Ongoing Basis

As implementation proceeds, you need to gather and evaluate data. Measurement results should reveal movement toward your goals for the new process. Are you making great headway? Evaluate process performance on an ongoing basis to determine the extent of your progress.

This step of the implementation phase requires that your team:

- Holds regular meetings
- Celebrates progress

Hold regular meetings

Your process-reengineering team should not disband as soon as implementation begins or even after it is over. Your meetings are still necessary, because you have to evaluate progress and take care of any problems that arise. Your meetings may be less frequent than before implementation, but they are still required.

To evaluate progress, you must analyze measurement data. You may want to use a tool, such as a Run Chart, to compare one period of data to another. It helps you verify whether your reengineered process has improved performance; and, if so, how much. To complete a Run Chart, you must determine what to measure, draw the graph, and plot the data.

The process-reengineering team at Shore Up...
committed to meeting weekly both during and after implementation. They were encouraged by the reaction of employees and customers alike. *"But we also need to see the facts that support our effort,"* Loudin said. Different team members volunteered to gather data on different measures. Shelley and Lonny offered to track resolutions of customer problems. Here is a sample of their Run Chart:

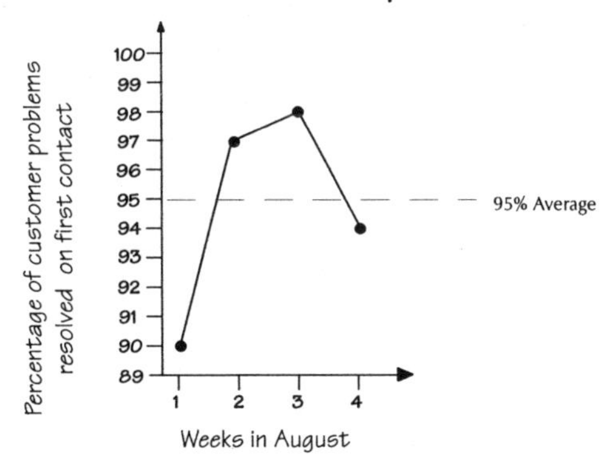

> *"We have made inroads in resolving customer problems,"* Loudin said, after distributing copies of the Run Chart to all members. *Next week, we'll look at other improvements."* ...

Also use your meetings to discuss any problems *(a likely scenario with any major reengineering effort).* Encourage team members to stay on top of problems by talking with employees to:

- Check to see that guidelines are being followed
- Uncover issues that need to be addressed
- Identify if extra support or resources are necessary to complete tasks
- Determine any obstacles that need to be removed
- See that quality service and/or products are being delivered

Depending on your process-reengineering effort, your team may meet for quite some time *(two years is not unheard of).* But there will come a time when you feel you are ready to move on and allow the process to be evaluated and continuously improved by the process *"owner(s)."* The new process is firmly established, your organization has reached its goal of dramatic improvement, and you and your team members could be used more effectively elsewhere. Knowing when to disband marks an effective process-reengineering team.

Celebrate progress

A successful process-reengineering effort deserves commendation. Reward all those who took part in helping your organization make the quantum leap toward radical improvement. Plan a formal celebration or informally recognize the winners in your organization. If you celebrate progress as it occurs, you'll increase commitment to your effort.

The enthusiasm at Shore Up...

was catching. The process-reengineering team made sure to post all increases in performance in the different departments. For example, on the wall near the customer representatives, Shelley and Joshua posted a banner stating: *"Customer Satisfaction Has Reached 95%!!! Thanks For Your Help!"* And Mark made sure all efforts were recognized in the company newsletter. Shore Up was no longer sinking below its competitors. The horizon looked bright.

The implementation phase is both exhilarating and exhausting. It takes time, but it can breathe new life into your organization. And that new life may be just what it needs to compete.

CHAPTER NINE WORKSHEET: PUTTING YOUR EFFORT TO THE TEST

1. Describe how you will implement your process-reengineering effort on a *"trial-run"* basis.

2. List the ways you will standardize your reengineered process.

3. How do you propose to evaluate your data?

4. How will you celebrate your success?

CHAPTER TEN

SUMMARY

Process reengineering has the potential to transform your organization. It can move an organization past its competitors, and place it in a position of optimal performance. But it does require strenuous work.

Following the Process-Reengineering Model is not easy, but what worthwhile quest ever is? Commitment to process reengineering may be the best investment your organization makes. The three phases—planning, designing, and implementing—will lift your organization from the groundwork of strategic planning, up through the trenches of designing a new process, to the heights of spectacular performance only achievable through careful implementation.

And after implementation? Your team's job is not yet complete. Every star performer knows that excellence lasts only if you continually work at it. The same is true for any organization that has dramatically increased its performance through process reengineering.

Strive to maintain an atmosphere of continuous process improvement *(CPI)*, and your reengineered process will continue to achieve breakthrough results. Use process reengineering and CPI as complementary approaches. Your organization will never be the same!

Reproducible Forms And Worksheets

The pages in the Appendix are provided for you to photocopy and use appropriately.

Role-Transition Worksheet

Role-Transition Worksheet			
Position Title:		Future Title:	
Present Responsibilities		Future Responsibilities	
Key Functions	Key Responsibilities	Additions (*) Deletions (-)	Targeted Results

Cost/Benefit Model

The Cost/Benefit Model consists of the following four steps:

1. Clarify Reengineering Option
2. Determine Cost/Benefit Categories
3. Gather Necessary Data
4. Calculate Cost/Benefit Relationship

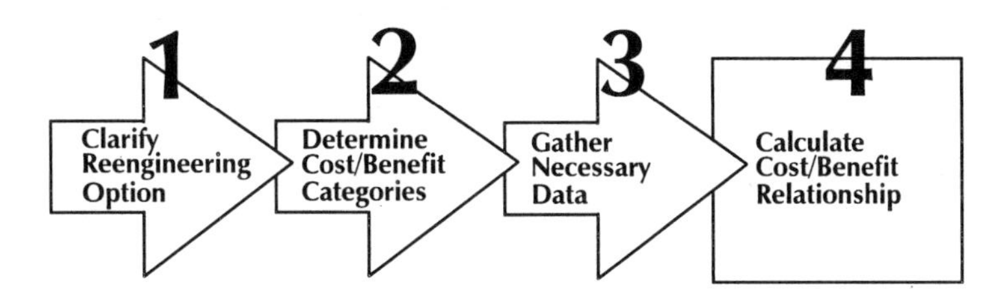

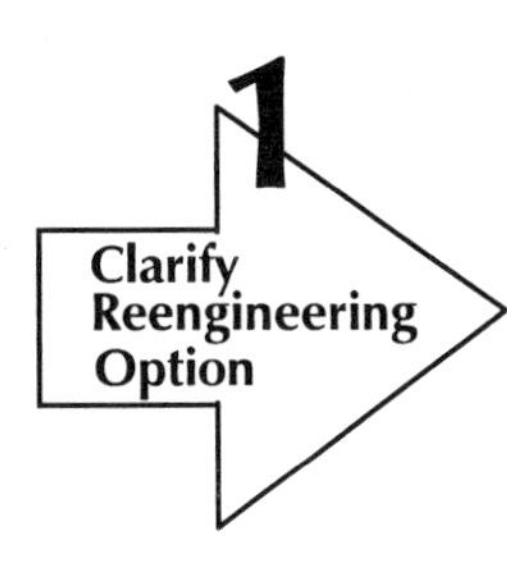

- Describe the proposed option
- Verify the option's link to specific organization-wide goals/Key Result Areas
- Summarize predicted/expected process performance gains
- Determine whether cost/benefit analysis is really worth doing *(Is an option already a given?, Is it too expensive to do cost/benefit analysis for this option?, Is it a politically influenced situation, for which cost/benefit analysis is just an exercise?, etc.)*
- Build *(and get sign-off if necessary)* a cost/benefit analysis project plan *(objectives, roles, deliverables, dates, etc.)*

- Locate similar, valid efforts to identify categories and line items; can lean on company archives, finance people, professional associations, other companies, resources such as libraries and on-line services
- Partner with knowledgeable people *(finance, subject-matter experts, workers close to the option, customers)* to brainstorm cost/benefit categories and line items; make it a team effort to ensure creative and comprehensive brainstorming and refining
- Refine categories and line items to final list; input on *"Cost/Benefit Calculation Worksheet"*

COST/BENEFIT MODEL

(continued)

- Use appropriate data gathering methods
- Document assumptions completely and accurately
- "Guesstimate" when necessary
- Project results as realistically as possible
- Calculate relational benefits where appropriate

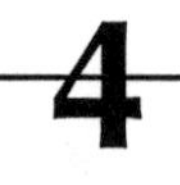

Calculate
Cost/Benefit
Relationship

- Project cost/benefit over appropriate time periods (*1 year, 2 years, etc.*)
- Consider contingencies
- When possible, develop three possible scenarios of cost/benefit analysis: Best, Probable, Worst
- Make sure as many possible "*what if's*" are considered and accounted for during analysis
- Avoid slanting, hiding, or inappropriately overemphasizing data
- List appropriate conclusion(s)/recommendation(s)

Cost/Benefit Calculation Worksheet

Scenario: ☐ Best ☑ Probable ☐ Worst

All figures are: ☑ Annual ☐ Monthly ☐ Other____________________

<table>
<tr><th colspan="3">Costs</th><th colspan="3">Benefits</th></tr>
<tr><th>Category/ Process Factor</th><th>Amount</th><th>Total</th><th>Category/ Process Factor</th><th>Amount</th><th>Total</th></tr>
<tr><td colspan="3"><u>Labor Category</u></td><td colspan="3"><u>Labor Category</u></td></tr>
<tr><td colspan="3"><u>Equipment/Materials Category</u></td><td colspan="3"><u>Equipment/Materials Category</u></td></tr>
<tr><td colspan="3"><u>Other Categories</u></td><td colspan="3"><u>Other Categories</u></td></tr>
<tr><td colspan="3">Totals Ongoing:
One-time:
Total:</td><td colspan="3">Totals Ongoing:
One-time:
Total:</td></tr>
</table>

COST/BENEFIT CALCULATION WORKSHEET *(continued)*

Comparison Of Costs And Benefits

	Year 1 (*One-time + Ongoing*)	Year 2+ (*Ongoing*)
Total Benefits=	$	$
Total Costs =	$	$
Difference ($Benefits – $Costs)=	$	$

(*If the difference is positive, the option being considered may be a viable one; however, the magnitude of the difference should be examined. See the section below.*)

Magnitude Of Difference

ROI = Return On Investment

$$\text{ROI} = \frac{\textit{return - investment}}{\textit{investment}} \times 100 = \frac{\$\_\_\_\_\_}{\$} \times 100 = \_\_\_\_\_\_\%$$

Where: ***return***=*benefits – ongoing costs*
investment=*one-time costs*

	By End Of Year 1	By End Of Year 2
$\text{ROI} = \frac{\textit{return - investment}}{\textit{investment}} \times 100 =$	$\frac{\$\_\_\_\_\_}{\$} \times 100$	$\frac{\$\_\_\_\_\_}{\$} \times 100$
=	$\frac{\$\_\_\_\_\_}{\$} \times 100$	$\frac{\$\_\_\_\_\_}{\$} \times 100$
=	_____ %	_____ %

Conclusion(s)/Recommendation(s)

TASK/ RESPONSIBILITY MATRIX

TASK/RESPONSIBILITY MATRIX							
	RESPONSIBILITY						
TASK							

PROCESS TASKS WORKSHEET

TASK #	MAJOR PROCESS TASKS	SUBTASKS/DECISIONS	SYMBOL

Action Plan

Action Plan					
Action Step/ Task	Responsible Person/Team	Begin Date	End Date	Est. Hours	Est. Cost

The Practical Guidebook Collection From Richard Chang Associates, Inc. Publications Division

Our Practical Guidebook Collection is growing to meet the challenges of the ever-changing workplace of the 90's. Look for these and other titles from Richard Chang Associates, Inc. on your bookstore shelves and in book catalogs.

Quality Improvement Series

- Meetings That Work!
- Continuous Improvement Tools Volume 1
- Continuous Improvement Tools Volume 2
- Step-By-Step Problem Solving
- Satisfying Internal Customers First!
- Continuous Process Improvement
- Improving Through Benchmarking
- Succeeding As A Self-Managed Team
- Process Reengineering In Action

Management Skills Series

- Coaching Through Effective Feedback
- Expanding Leadership Impact
- Mastering Change Management
- On-The-Job Orientation And Training
- Re-Creating Teams During Transitions

High Performance Team Series

- Success Through Teamwork
- Team Decision-Making Techniques
- Measuring Team Performance
- Building A Dynamic Team

High-Impact Training Series

- Creating High-Impact Training
- Identifying Targeted Training Needs
- Mapping A Winning Training Approach
- Producing High-Impact Learning Tools
- Applying Successful Training Techniques
- Measuring The Impact Of Training
- Make Your Training Results Last

ADDITIONAL RESOURCES FROM RICHARD CHANG ASSOCIATES, INC.

Evaluation And Feedback Form

In order to continuously improve the quality of the resources provided through Richard Chang Associates, Inc., Publications Division, we need your help. We would greatly appreciate your input and suggestions regarding this particular guidebook, as well as future guidebook interests.

Please photocopy this form before completing, since other readers may use this guidebook. Thank you in advance for your feedback.

Guidebook Title: ____

1. Overall, how would you rate your *level of satisfaction* with this guidebook? Please circle your response.

Extremely Dissatisfied		Satisfied		Extremely Satisfied
1	2	3	4	5

2. What specific *concepts or methods* did you find <u>*most*</u> helpful?

____

____

3. What specific *concepts or methods* did you find <u>*least*</u> helpful?

____

____

4. As an individual who may purchase additional guidebooks in the future, what *characteristics/features/benefits* are most important to you in making a decision to purchase a guidebook *(or another similar book)*?

____

____

5. What additional *subject matter/topic areas* would you like to see available as a guidebook in the future?

____

____

Name *(optional)*: ____

Address: ____

C/S/Z: ______________________ **Phone (   )** ______________________

Please Fax Your Responses To: (714) 756-0853